Maker Innovations Series

Jump start your path to discovery with the Apress Maker Innovations series! From the basics of electricity and components through to the most advanced options in robotics and Machine Learning, you'll forge a path to building ingenious hardware and controlling it with cutting-edge software. All while gaining new skills and experience with common toolsets you can take to new projects or even into a whole new career.

The Apress Maker Innovations series offers projects-based learning, while keeping theory and best processes front and center. So you get hands-on experience while also learning the terms of the trade and how entrepreneurs, inventors, and engineers think through creating and executing hardware projects. You can learn to design circuits, program AI, create IoT systems for your home or even city, and so much more!

Whether you're a beginning hobbyist or a seasoned entrepreneur working out of your basement or garage, you'll scale up your skillset to become a hardware design and engineering pro. And often using low-cost and open-source software such as the Raspberry Pi, Arduino, PIC microcontroller, and Robot Operating System (ROS). Programmers and software engineers have great opportunities to learn, too, as many projects and control environments are based in popular languages and operating systems, such as Python and Linux.

If you want to build a robot, set up a smart home, tackle assembling a weather-ready meteorology system, or create a brand-new circuit using breadboards and circuit design software, this series has all that and more! Written by creative and seasoned Makers, every book in the series tackles both tested and leading-edge approaches and technologies for bringing your visions and projects to life.

More information about this series at https://link.springer.com/bookseries/17311.

Ultimate LEGO Worldbuilding and Architecture

How to Create Anything with Speedy Techniques at a Low Price

Mark Rollins

Apress®

Ultimate LEGO Worldbuilding and Architecture: How to Create Anything with Speedy Techniques at a Low Price

Mark Rollins
Pullman, WA, USA

ISBN-13 (pbk): 979-8-8688-0520-2   ISBN-13 (electronic): 979-8-8688-0521-9
https://doi.org/10.1007/979-8-8688-0521-9

Copyright © 2024 by Mark Rollins

Managing Director, Apress Media LLC: Welmoed Spahr
Acquisitions Editor: Miriam Haidara
Development Editor: James Markham
Project Manager: Jessica Vakili

Cover designed by eStudioCalamar

Distributed to the book trade worldwide by Apress Media, LLC, 1 New York Plaza, New York, NY 10004, U.S.A. Phone 1-800-SPRINGER, fax (201) 348-4505, e-mail orders-ny@springer-sbm.com, or visit www.springeronline.com. Apress Media, LLC is a California LLC and the sole member (owner) is Springer Science + Business Media Finance Inc (SSBM Finance Inc). SSBM Finance Inc is a **Delaware** corporation.

For information on translations, please e-mail booktranslations@springernature.com; for reprint, paperback, or audio rights, please e-mail bookpermissions@springernature.com.

Apress titles may be purchased in bulk for academic, corporate, or promotional use. eBook versions and licenses are also available for most titles. For more information, reference our Print and eBook Bulk Sales web page at http://www.apress.com/bulk-sales.

Any source code or other supplementary material referenced by the author in this book is available to readers on GitHub (https://github.com/Apress). For more detailed information, please visit https://www.apress.com/gp/services/source-code.

If disposing of this product, please recycle the paper

Table of Contents

About the Author

 **Mark Rollins** has been an established writer for two decades, delving into tech and gadget blogging 20 years ago, contributing to various consumer electronics-related websites. Over the last 15 years, he has successfully managed TheGeekChurch.com, boasting a tech website, a YouTube channel (700+ subscribers), and a TikTok channel (20,000+ followers). As a seasoned author, Mark has published six books with Apress, covering Android Marketing, LEGO, Kindle Fire, and UBTECH/Jimu Robots, displaying a diverse and comprehensive writing portfolio.

About the Technical Reviewer

Farzin Asadi received his B.Sc. in Electronics Engineering, his M.Sc. in Control Engineering, and his Ph.D. in Mechatronics Engineering. Currently, he is with the Department of Electrical and Electronics Engineering at the Maltepe University, Istanbul, Turkey. Dr. Asadi has published over 40 international papers and 29 books. He is on the editorial board of seven scientific journals as well. His research interests include switching converters, control theory, robust control of power electronics converters, and robotics.

CHAPTER 1

LEGO: Past, Present, and Future

Introduction

I received my first LEGO set as a Christmas present when I was in first grade, and I remember looking at it with no knowledge of what LEGO even was. This particular set was a Universal Building Set, and there were pictures all over the box to show what you could build with it. Like most kids, I started building by imitating what was on the box, but even with the limitations of imitation, it became very apparent that the potential of building with LEGO was absolutely limitless. The more I grew up, the more I realized that I could achieve greater satisfaction from building something that I created from the ground up or, in many cases, from the LEGO baseplate up.

Now that I am much older (in my 50s), I am grateful to discover that I'm not the only adult who still appreciates the infinite properties of building with LEGO. There are some adults that believe that LEGO should stay left behind in our childhoods, but there are some adults who still consider it important and will still make the time in their busy adult lives to create with it. That is really what building with LEGO is all about: creation.

© Mark Rollins 2024
M. Rollins, *Ultimate LEGO Worldbuilding and Architecture*, Maker Innovations Series,
https://doi.org/10.1007/979-8-8688-0521-9_1

What I Want You to Get from This Book (the Takeaway)

You who are reading this book, I want to say that I have no idea how old you are, but I want to emphasize how LEGO is a tool for creating worlds. Now you might ask, why should we want to create a world, isn't there already a world there that has been created that we can live in? A world that has its own versions of LEGO pieces in the form of resources so we can build up to be that which we want it to be? To that I say: have you tried living in it?

I'm going to just say it: LEGO is a distraction. Just like the author who writes a book, the painter who makes a portrait, the sculptor who crafts a statue, the end result may not change the world in any way and could be seen as a time waster. However, no one can truthfully say that some pieces of art haven't touched their lives, and I will assure that every creation has changed the creator in some form, usually for the better.

Author Irene Claremont de Catillejo has stated: "Nothing is more satisfying to the human soul than creating something new." After all, most of us spend a lot of time in our own world, working just to provide for ourselves in our jobs in an effort just to survive. Sometimes we need a break from it, and could use an activity that rewards our creativity and not our repetition.

One of the things that makes LEGO so satisfying is that you are taking something that looks broken in its first form and making it whole. Each LEGO set is just a pile of pieces until you start putting it together, and then, it becomes something extraordinary, something that, at the very least, was not there before.

You may have discovered LEGO as a child and discovered there is fun in putting things together. Maybe part of it is to shun chaos and put something into order with the help of a little bit of instruction. If you are the type that purchases LEGO just so you can assemble it and put it on the shelf, like art, I fully support this, provided that you can support yourself.

However, if you are like most LEGO enthusiasts, you don't want to just follow a set of instructions, even if it would make it easier to put some ideas (but not your own) into form. You might not even know exactly what you want to build, only you just have to do it. However, you might not have the right amount of pieces, and these are the problems that I would like to address in this first chapter.

I'm going to be talking about how to build whatever you want to build, using the bricks that LEGO can provide, and I also want to give some advice on how you can affordably get more pieces for the creations that you want to make.

I'm also going to show you the best ways for building, and part of it is the maintenance of sorting. Yes, I also enjoy the whole aspect of sorting through much LEGO, but when you are building, you don't want to be spending all your time looking for one particular piece.

So yes, I will teach you about sorting, but this series will also bring you lessons about what you really want to do: building. I'll start you off on how to make a solid foundation for your creation (whatever it might be) and then how to populate it with realistic buildings and vehicles. Then, I want to talk about things that require more imagination, like spaceships, robots, and other mythical beasts. Not only will you learn to create it, but you will make it stand strong and not fall apart so easily.

I'll give you a brief introduction of myself. My name is Mark Rollins, and I have been building with LEGO since I was young and continued to do it long after others told me that I shouldn't. I have written two books about LEGO Technic and one about another type of programmable LEGO, LEGO MINDSTORMS EV3.

In addition to this book about LEGO Worldbuilding, I am also writing a book about how to build with LEGO Technic, which should be released at the same time as this book. For those who are not in the know, LEGO Technic is a type of construction that emphasizes more mechanized forms and larger scale models. So if you are also interested in building with LEGO

Technic, which I only slightly mention in this book, check that one out! But enough of my self-promotion. I want to help you with your LEGO building experience, no matter where you are at. Let's just get started building!

The History of LEGO

I thought it would be fun to discuss the history of LEGO and all of its iterations before getting into it. I know I had a lot of fun just looking at old LEGO catalogs, some of them that I still had with me since my childhood.

When it comes to who founded LEGO, it gets attributed to Ole Kirk Kristiansen in 1932 (Figure 1-1), and this family-owned business has been passed down from father to son. I believe that his name was actually "Ole," and this is not a reference to his age, even though he looks pretty old from this photo of him that I found online.

Figure 1-1. *Ole Kirk Kristiansen, the creator of LEGO as we know it*

You will notice that LEGO is often used in all capitals, but it is not an acronym. It stems from two Danish words meaning "play well," and it also means "I put together" in Latin. The LEGO name was officially used in 1936, but only on their highly crafted wooden toys, and it wasn't until ten years later when the Kristiansen family invests in plastic.

In about 1949, the LEGO bricks begin to look like what they are now, somewhat. Think of the basic 2 × 4 brick, but empty on the bottom, and you have it.

Figure 1-2. *The first LEGO bricks, which look only slightly different from the LEGO bricks of today*

These pieces were called the Automatic Binding Brick, and the original catalog from that year has some of the early sets, which were small houses that looked very blocky, sort of like Minecraft. These houses had roofs that did not slope, but there were already window-like pieces that appeared to show off what type of detail these early LEGO construction sets were capable of.

Figure 1-3. *An early catalog of LEGO, with the name of "Automatic Binding Bricks"*

By 1953, the LEGO name appears on every brick, just like it appears on every stud (the round section of the brick), with construction kits of LEGO Mursten (LEGO bricks) to encourage creative play. LEGO drops the name of Automatic Binding Bricks and began to produce brochures that showed models that could be produced from extra sets. In 1955, there was a town plan that had bricks of all kinds of interesting shapes, even with curves. There are vehicles on these catalogs, but it doesn't look like the user could assemble these like the buildings. The vehicles looked more like Matchbox or Hot Wheels cars.

It wasn't until 1958 that the coupling principle is patented, which really highlights the "clicking together" that LEGO is truly known for. It was very apparent that the family realized its potential and encouraged building up of LEGO bricks in order to stimulate children's creativity.

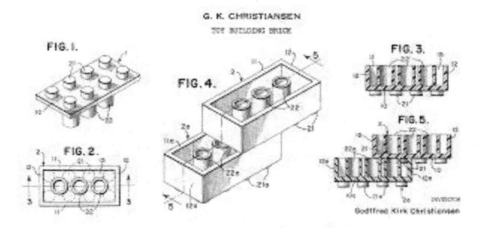

Figure 1-4. *The patent for LEGO's "click together" technology*

Then in 1960, a fire destroys the company's wooden toy warehouse, which marks the time when LEGO begins to stop production of their wooden toys. The LEGO toys begin to flourish, with wheeled creations in 1962, and by 1965, new catalogs begin to come out each year that highlight the growth of the company. In fact, if you want to see how much LEGO has grown in the past 60 years, I highly recommend going through their old catalogs. Much of the information that I could find came from the ones that I found online or the ones that I had in my own collection. I recommend looking at this website at BrickSet: `https://brickset.com/library/catalogues`.

Figure 1-5. *Samples of LEGO trucks in 1968. These models look very archaic compared to what LEGO has now, but it shows a progression*

An early catalog from 1966 shows that the company was heavily marketing basic sets with Playpacks such as basic set 070 (LEGO set numbers are now in the tens of thousands). Sets started to have a little more detail with the introduction of sloped or "bevelled" bricks. Even in the mid- to late 1960s, LEGO had motorized parts, particularly with trains. Granted, the trains and cars were very rudimentary in their designs.

By 1968, the vehicles became a little bit more detailed, as a possible prototype to the Technic/modeling team. There are tipper trucks with hinge pieces and a truck with a crane. This begins bricks with functions, even if they were not mechanical. It's interesting to see the scale that differs from the buildings to the vehicles.

By the way, 1968 is when Legoland opened in Bilund, Denmark, and it had 10 acres of very elaborately constructed LEGO houses. That really must have been a great sight to see, even now. It is 1969 where Duplo is unveiled, but I'm not going to cover that series much in this book. Just to let you know, the Duplo is twice the size of a LEGO brick in all dimensions. The Duplo can also be used in construction for when you need, but I'll talk about that later.

Anyway, in 1970, the Town sets began to look to scale with their miniature LEGO cars. In 1971, the company created "dolls furniture sets specially for girls," which had kitchens and dining room tables that were more than a few bricks high, too big for the towns that they were also marketing.

In 1973, these basic sets are created, presumably with a new numbering system. The Town sets were getting more complex, and there is even a rocket base that predates the space system by several years. The LEGO boats become available, and they can really float.

In 1974, LEGO realized that they needed to add people, so the LEGO family was introduced. These first LEGO people are very large compared to the minifig. The plan was to use them with the doll furniture.

In 1976, the basic sets get a double-digit upgrade with 10, 20, 30, 40, and 50. The sets also become a bit more advanced as well, and I remember having the 402 set. They start doing models based on more real things like the Spirit of St. Louis and a Boeing 727. Also, this is when these figures start to appear. They were just these guys with no faces and cutoff stubs for arms. Their feet did not move, but they had hats.

Figure 1-6. *The minifigs, with the first two in its first iteration and the second two with the design that is still used today*

Sometime in 1978 and 1979, Kjeld Kirk Kristiansen starts this "system within the system," which is made to offer the right products to the right age. This is when a lot of new things start happening.

This is when the new improved minifigure steps in, and it works with the Town system, phasing out those stiff other armless and fused leg guys. It also opens the door for the Expert sets, which is a subject of another book that I have written about Technic. I'll focus the rest of this LEGO history lesson on sets that are of the minifig scale, but I do talk a lot about LEGO Technic history in the aforementioned other LEGO Technic book.

In 1979, a very big event happens as LEGO unveils Space. I don't think it is any coincidence that this set showed up a few years after *Star Wars*. LEGO Space definitely sets its sights on the stars, fitting for the space age and beyond.

Figure 1-7. *The LEGO Space system, one of their most successful programs, ever*

Oh, there was also Fabuland. A series that didn't really take off, which has happened several times throughout the history of LEGO, and I am most certain that there are entire series that I left out of this history. However, the Castle system, which appears as kind of an afterthought in the catalog, really took off.

The minifigs also really made the towns come to life as the buildings now felt liveable, some of them opening up to reveal more on the inside.

These Town, Space, Knights, and other sets were enough for LEGO to advertise as "toys you grow up with" and "the toy children add to, rather than outgrow." Speaking of growing, they really bought the whole train thing back with a set made for the town scale.

Figure 1-8. *An ad campaign for LEGO to show how it was marketed as "toys you grow up with"*

In 1988, LEGO added the Light and Sound, the first time they used light and sound on their bricks. In 1989, another very popular system was introduced with the new Pirates collections, with the very elaborate boats with sails and character faces that were more than just yellow with a smiley.

Like the whole "system with a system," the LEGO Space was one of those collections that had different series within them and usually only lasting a few years before being discontinued. LEGO attempted the Space Police and with a monorail system. They also have Futuron and Blacktron, different variations of the Space sets. The 1990s saw the addition of the M:TRON, where magnets were used to lock certain bricks into place. There was also the Ice Planet sets, made for a planet with ice.

The Knights system also had its systems within, and the Knights collection grew with Forestmen, which were guys who lived in the forest like Robin Hood. And there were also glow-in-the-dark ghosts. The Knights system had a kind of shift in its modeling as there were a lot of dependence on pre-fab pieces rather than individual bricks. The shift in bigger pieces made it easier to build, but many builders wondered what else could be done with them once the initial set was created.

The Towns systems also had their own collections within collections like Flight, Max RPM, Nautica, and RSQ 911. In 1992, Octan came to town, a fictitious big oil company that appears on a lot of LEGO systems.

There was a shift in 1992 to make some more girl-friendly models, something that LEGO had been kind of shifting away from. There was Paradisa in 1993, which had more pastel pinks to make it like Barbie's beach paradise. By 1994, it went to Belville, which had some very larger dolls in it. These types of sets still exist in the form of the LEGO Friends series.

The other types of sets came to be more advanced with new types of pieces being created annually. Boats still kept floating, and trains got pretty advanced. The company continued its growth, with excellent marketing programs such as Zack and Jack the LEGO Maniac.

Figure 1-9. *Jack (originally called Zack) the LEGO Maniac, the spokesperson for LEGO in the 1980s and 1990s*

There were always advances to each of the sets in some form. For example, the Pirates had these Imperial Guards in 1993. In 1994, there were the Islanders, which might be considered culturally insensitive. The Knights in 1993 had Dragon Masters, Wolfpack, and Black Knights. Then, in 1995, there were the Royal Knights and the Dark Forest. In the Space systems, it turned to Spyrius; then, 1994 brought Unitron. Then, 1995 bought Exporiens. It was 1995 that brought in Aquazone, bringing LEGO underwater as good as it could with the Aquanauts and Aquasharks.

It was in 1997 where things got really shaken up; LEGO brought in RoboForce, UFO, Fright Knights, and Aquazone with Aqua Raiders. These were all new set systems, very different than the ones before. LEGO also tried new types of sets with Outback and Wild West. There was also the very weird one with Time Twisters, kind of a surreal set devoted to time-travelling characters.

Figure 1-10. *LEGO had an explosion of new sets in 1997*

One year later, 1998 brought in Adventurers, think Indiana Jones, but without the Indiana Jones. There was also Insectoids for Space. Aquazone branched out with Hydronauts and Stingrays. LEGO brought out the Ninjas, which was not the Ninjago sets, as they would come later. There was also the Res Q, a team with black vehicles that did rescues. Since it was the 1990s, there was the Xtreme Team, because it was the 1990s, everything was marketed as extreme back then.

Then, since it was 1999, the year of the long-anticipated *Star Wars: Episode I*, LEGO got *Star Wars*-related toys, which is one of their most successful collections to this day. There was also Rock Raiders, which was not so successful. The Town had more become the City Center, and these sets have been rebranded to just "City" from now on and continues with new models today.

There was also a wide variety of LEGO software. They were for the console games or PC, and I remember the Creator software, but I'll discuss LEGO Creation software in later chapters. In 2000, there was MINDSTORMS. This was an intelligent brick playset that I write about more in my LEGO Technic book as well as my earlier work about *Beginning LEGO MINDSTORMS EV3*.

The 2000s was an interesting time as set systems would come and go. There was this MyBot system which allowed for creativity with different functions. Scala, targeted for younger girls, started showing up as well. There was also a brief stint of Arctic sets, kind of an offshoot of the Ice Planet sets without the space factor. Sports finally got into the action with LEGO soccer fields.

In 2001, there was LEGO Race and the Alpha Team Spy group, a kind of espionage action themed set that was popular for a while. There was also a studio collaboration with Steven Spielberg where LEGO builders could apply their talent to making movies, thanks to a specialized camera (this was before every phone had a camera, and every phone became a smartphone). LEGO was always trying to be ahead of its time, and many times, they succeeded.

The Town and Knights sets continued to grow, and Space had shifted more toward *Star Wars*, but LEGO also had the Life on Mars thing as well. Then, there was the Bionicle, which was first introduced under the Technic umbrella, but these sets really grew in popularity over the years, with some made-to-DVD movies.

Figure 1-11. *LEGO Harry Potter, one of their more popular systems, debuting in 2001 with the launch of the first film*

Then in 2002, this was when LEGO Harry Potter came around, which also became a huge hit. There was also the Dinosaurs systems. Does anyone remember Jack Stone? Because that was a thing. Then, Mission Alpha went Deep Sea, so I guess the Aquanauts were out? Yes, there were times where LEGO would focus on a new thing and king of forget the old thing, like how Knights sort of took a backburner to Harry Potter, and Classic Space got essentially shelved due to the still-continuing popularity of *Star Wars*.

Even though the 1990s were over, 2003 has an Island Extreme sets with skateboarders. Oh, then, there was the Orient Expedition, which had these big domed roofs and other things not really seen in LEGO before. Sports got an expansion with basketball and hockey. Oh, there was also Spybiotics and then the big fail of Galidor, which has been reported as one of LEGO's biggest failures.

By 2004, there was an attempt to appeal to girls again with Clikits. The Knights Kingdom began, with large figures that were kind of similar to Bionicle. Oh, and *Spider-Man 2* had a set, one of LEGO's first forays into super-hero-related IP.

At some point, LEGO had developed a Creator system that still is around. Creator, particularly the sets with the 3-in-1 building products, is a really good jumping-off point for any LEGO enthusiast old and young and is often cheaper than some of the other licensed sets.

Speaking of licensed sets, it is in 2007 where *Batman* shows up. It is 2008 which has a nice Model Town House, and these detailed town houses are still available on LEGO current catalogs and have a lot of great details. Indiana Jones sets also start to come out (since *Indiana Jones and the Kingdom of the Crystal Skull* bought Indy back in theaters), and one set that I thought should have done better than its initial movie release: *Speed Racer*.

Yes, LEGO would often back some franchise, and oftentimes, it might not pay off. For example, 2010 had *Prince of Persia* sets. Does anyone even remember the *Prince of Persia* movie? LEGO would often try other things that were similar to other ones of the past like the 2009 Power Miners that looked a lot like Rock Raiders.

By 2011, LEGO realized it had a hit with Ninjago, and this still exists. They also started producing licensed sets with Disney's *Pirates of the Caribbean*, and this kind of eclipsed the whole Pirates sets that they had been doing for a while.

By 2014, the year that hit *The Lego Movie* was released, there were all kinds of sets related to IP like Ninja Turtles, both Marvel and DC, Minecraft, Lord of the Rings, and even Minecraft, because (let's face it) these two are kind of related. I had almost forgotten about Ultra Agents and Chima.

Since this is getting very long, and you have a good idea of the diversity of LEGO's products throughout the decades, I will quickly summarize the last decade. You can see their current catalog still has a lot of material related to popular sets as City, Ninjago, *Star Wars*, Minecraft, and Harry

Potter, and even Jurassic Park has shown up. There is also newer sets like Sonic the Hedgehog and Mario, video games which have had great success in their big-screen adaptations.

There has also been an increase in Speed, a series devoted to making car models that is separate from Technic, which is also still produced by LEGO. At some point, there was also an emphasis in LEGO Architecture, sets that are very different from the minifig scale sets and Technic sets, but really showcase modern marvels. I'll talk more about LEGO Architecture in the next chapter.

Something that has been very big for LEGO recently has been its flower collection. Since this book focuses more about creating in a minifig scale, I won't be discussing anything about LEGO flowers.

Okay, so that was a cool look back through history! Maybe that brought back memories from when you were a kid, about all the models that you had, and maybe those that you couldn't afford to get back then.

For me, there were a lot that I couldn't afford, and since I wanted them all, I began to realize that I had better make with what I had. Most of us probably had a friend or neighbor who had a lot of sets, and I remember one friend of mine who had built a LEGO Space mothership that was 4 feet long. I thought it was one of the coolest things that I had ever seen, but I'm very certain that with the LEGO pieces that I had at the time, I couldn't make something like that. However, if this is the time to really start making your LEGO dreams come to life, you still might need a few more LEGO bricks to make that happen.

Places to Purchase LEGO Bricks Affordably

Yes, if you wanted to increase the amount of LEGO bricks you have, you could go to the LEGO store or LEGO online and max our your credit cards, but hey, stop trying to do that!

I'm going to show you in this book how to build big, and the emphasis is going to be on using pieces that you probably have already, and if you are just looking for pieces, I can tell you where you can get some for a very cheap price.

If you are like me, then you have accrued a lot of LEGO pieces throughout your lifetime. Most parents who have become empty nesters admit that they have Rubbermaid totes full of LEGO bricks, and if their kids have outgrown them, they don't want to just throw away. Some will just give them away.

Just go on online auctions, as there are probably a few that you have unknowingly subscribed to on Facebook. There's also sites like Craigslist, and when I checked the "For Sale" section under "toys and games," there was an explosion of LEGO.

I was curious if these particular sets that I found on Craigslist were new and did a search on LEGO to find that it was a retired product. I then did a search for it on eBay and found the price even lower if I wanted to buy it used. That meant that there would not be the original box or instructions, but at least I could find the instructions online.

If you are one of those LEGO enthusiasts that wants to keep the box of every set that you ever owned, all I have to say to that is: you must have a lot of storage space. I'm not into collecting for the sake of cashing it in for a higher value, but I'm going to guess that if you actually have a set from the 1960s or 1970s that is somehow unopened, you might want to sell it for a lot so you can get a lot for money for bricks.

In many cases, you might be able to find a whole lot of bricks just stuffed in some Rubbermaid tote. I think we all know the life of LEGO is a toy that a child might play with for a while until they grow up. Of course, those sets can be pretty up there in price, so in many cases, the parents just box them up, because they don't want to just chuck them in the garbage.

So yes, they would be willing to simply give away piles of LEGO bricks just to save on space, and it is the easiest and lowest price way of obtaining more LEGO pieces for building. The problem is it is like that box of chocolates, and you never know what you are going to get.

If you are looking for more specific pieces, which might happen when you are doing more elaborate builds, there are also many sites available for that, such as Bricklink. Again, prices will vary and I will discuss specific LEGO pieces you may need later in this chapter.

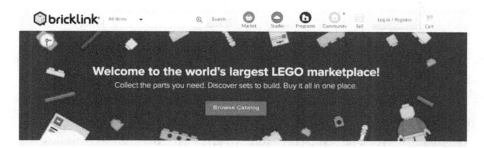

Figure 1-12. *Website for Bricklink, a place to really get LEGO at a good price*

Assuming you have access to lots of bricks, it becomes difficult to figure out what to build if you do not have any idea of what you have. Therefore, you have to learn to sort your bricks.

Sorting Bricks

So, there are several ways to sort bricks, and I highly recommend that you do, because it will just come in handy when you really need to find the brick that you are looking for when you need it. Most LEGO enthusiasts, or Master Builders, have a system of sorting which involves a lot of drawers. That is, small drawers that are the size of the ones on tackleboxes.

If you have a large collection, you could start by taking your pile of pieces and sorting them out by color. Granted, many modern-day LEGO pieces come in a wide variety of them, as there are several shades of blue, red, and yellow, not to mention the secondary colors.

However, I would recommend sorting by categories, and by categories, this relates to the shape of the LEGO piece and what it is made for. These are the ones that I would like to specify.

Bricks

If you were to just say "LEGO," these types of pieces are probably the first thing that comes to mind. The first ones that most kids play with, after Duplo, are ones that are two studs wide. After a while, kids get to using bricks just one stud wide, and these bricks come in many different lengths and widths.

By the way, I use "Pieces" to refer to any particular LEGO building block, but I will use the term block to any piece that is a certain size using a measurement of M to refer to one stud length.

Just to add another disclaimer, but in many of these collections of pieces illustrations that I show in this chapter, some of these types of pieces might not be available in that color. I often took some liberties when it came to coloring them so they would stand out. I'll talk more about the color of LEGO pieces in the next chapter.

You will note that every LEGO piece has a different ID number, included in the (parentheticals).

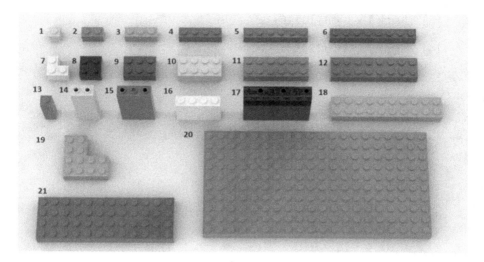

Figure 1-13. *Samples of LEGO bricks*

1) Brick 1 × 1 (3005)

2) Brick 1 × 2 (3004)

3) Brick 1 × 3 (3622)

4) Brick 1 × 4 (3010)

5) Brick 1 × 6 (3009)

6) Brick 1 × 8 (3008)

7) Brick 2 × 2 corner (2357)

8) Brick 2 × 2 (3003)

9) Brick 2 × 3 (3002)

10) Brick 2 × 4 (3001)

11) Brick 2 × 6 (2456)

12) Brick 2 × 8 (3007)

13)   Brick $1 \times 1 \times 3$ (14716)

14)   Brick $1 \times 2 \times 5$ (2454)

15)   Brick $1 \times 3 \times 5$ (3755)

16)   Brick $1 \times 4 \times 3$ (49311)

17)   Brick $1 \times 6 \times 5$ (3756)

18)   Brick 2×10 (3006)

19)   Brick 4×4 corner (702)

20)   Brick 10×20 (700ex)

21)   Brick 4×12 (4202)

Brick, Round

Just because it is a LEGO brick, it does not mean that it is square, and there are plenty of LEGO bricks that are round or rounded. This is a sample of a few that you will find.

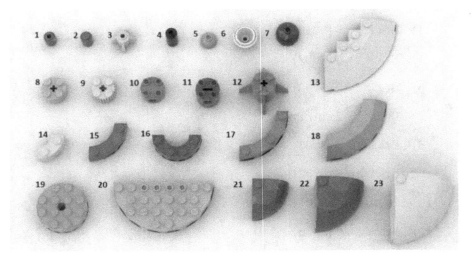

Figure 1-14. *Samples of round bricks*

1) Brick, round 1 × 1 (3062): The smallest of the round bricks at 1 × 1, think of it as a minifigure can.

2) Brick, round solid stud 1 × 1 (3062old): This is a round brick with no lip around the top and bottom.

3) Brick, round 1 × 1 with fins (4588).

4) Brick, round 1 × 1 × 1 2/3 (71075).

5) Brick, round 1 1/2 × 1 1/2 × 2/3 dome top (20952).

6) Brick, round 2 × 2 dome bottom (15395).

7) Brick, round 2 × 2 dome top (553b).

8) Brick, round 2 × 2 with axle hole (3941): I don't really discuss Technic axles in this book, but this piece will accommodate them.

9) Brick, round 2 × 2 with axle hole ribbed (92947).

10) Brick, round 2 × 2 with connector peg holes (17485): I don't discuss Technic connector pegs/pins in this book, but this piece can fit them.

11) Brick, round 2 × 2 × 2 with connector peg holes (30361c).

12) Brick, round 2 × 2 × 2 with fins (4591).

13) Brick, round corner 6 × 6 slope 33 edge (95188): This unusual piece has a curved wedge and corners on the other side.

14) Brick, round corner 2 × 2 (3063): If you were to put four of these together, it will form a circle.

15) Brick, round corner 3 × 3 (5152).

16) Brick, round corner 4 × 2 (x1042b): Two of these pieces can form a circle.

17) Brick, round corner 4 × 4 (48092).

18) Brick, round corner 5 × 5 slope 45 without studs (76795).

19) Brick, round 4 × 4 with hole (87081).

20) Brick, round corner 4 × 8 full brick double (47974).

21) Brick, round corner 3 × 3 × 2 dome top (88293): This piece can be combined with three others to make an interesting circular top.

22) Brick, round corner 4 × 4 × 2 2/3 dome top (49612).

23) Brick, round corner 5 × 5 × 3 1/3 dome top (76776).

Round Cones

In addition to some bricks being round, some of them are pointed as well. These are a few that I will point out on this.

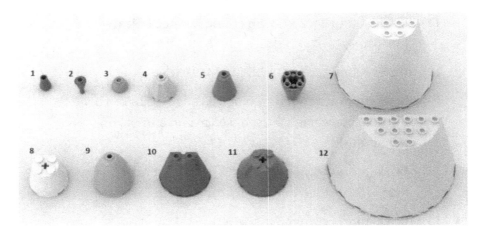

Figure 1-15. *Samples of the round cone bricks*

1) Cone 1 × 1 (4589)

2) Cone 1 × 1 inverted with bar (11610)

3) Cone 1 1/2 × 1 1/2 × 2/3 (33492)

4) Cone 2 × 2 × 1 2/3 octagonal (6039)

5) Cone 2 × 2 × 2 (3942b)

6) Cone 2 × 2 × 2 inverted (49309)

7) Cone half 8 × 4 × 6 (47543)

8) Cone 3 × 3 × 2 (6233)

9) Cone 3 × 3 × 3 elliptic paraboloid (1744)

10) Cone half 4 × 2 × 3 (38317)

11) Cone 4 × 4 × 2 with axle hole (3943b)

12) Cone half 10 × 5 × 6 (29096)

Bricks Modified

Occasionally, some bricks have a certain feature on them, hence the modified bricks. Some of these are made so the studs are on the side, which can bring about some very interesting forms.

Figure 1-16. *Samples of modified bricks*

1) Brick, Modified 1 × 3 with 3 loudspeakers (3963)

2) Brick, Modified 1 × 1 with bar handle (2921)

3) Brick, Modified 1 × 1 with clip horizontal (60476)

4) Brick, Modified 1 × 1 with open U clip (60475)

5) Brick, Modified 1 × 1 with headlight (4070)

6) Brick, Modified 1 × 1 with studs on 4 sides (4733)

7) Brick, Modified 1 × 1 × 1 2/3 with studs on the side (32952)

8) Brick, Modified 1 × 1 × 3 with 2 clips (60583b)

9) Brick, Modified 1 × 1 × 2/3 with studs on sides and extended stud receptacle (4595)

10) Brick, Modified 1 × 2 × 5 with channel (88393)

11) Brick, Modified facet 2 × 2 (87620)

12) Brick, Modified 1 × 2 with bar handle on the side (30236)

13) Brick, Modified 1 × 2 with channel (4216)

14) Brick, Modified 1 × 2 ribbed (2877)

15) Brick, Modified 1 × 2 with log profile (30136)

16) Brick, Modified 1 × 2 with open O clip thick (30237b)

17) Brick, Modified 1 × 2 with connector peg (44865)

18) Brick, Modified 1 × 2 with connector pegs (30526)

19) Brick, Modified 1 × 2 with studs on 1 side (11211)

20) Brick, Modified facet 3 × 3 (2462)

21) Brick, Modified 1 × 2 × 1 2/3 with studs and ends (67329)

22) Brick, Modified 1 × 4 with channel (2653)

23) Brick, Modified 1 × 4 with masonry profile (15533)

24) Brick, Modified 1 × 4 with studs on side (30414)

25) Brick, Modified 1 × 4 × 2 center stud top (4088)

26) Brick, Modified 1 × 4 with log profile (30137)

27) Brick, Modified facet 4 × 4 (14413)

28) Brick, Modified octagonal 2 × 2 × 3 1/3 (6037)

29) Brick, Modified octagonal 2 × 2 × 3 1/3 corner (6043)

30) Brick, Modified octagonal 2 × 2 × 3 1/3 with side studs (6042)

31) Brick, Modified 2 × 4 × 2 with studs on sides (2434)

32) Brick, Modified 2 × 4 × 2 with holes on sides (6061)

33) Brick, Modified facet 3 × 3 × 2 bottom (2464)

34) Brick, Modified facet 3 × 3 × 2 top (2463)

Arches

These types of pieces are good in case you want some realistic curves in your creation, as arch formations are very common in real architecture and can give architectural strength to a creation.

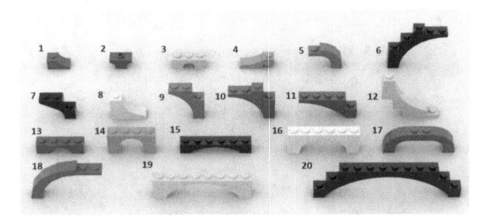

Figure 1-17. *Samples of LEGO arch pieces*

1) Arch 1 × 2 inverted (78666)

2) Arch 1 × 2 jumper (38583)

3) Arch 1 × 3 (4490)

4) Arch 1 × 3 inverted (70681)

5) Arch 1 × 3 × 2 curved top (6005)

6) Arch 1 × 5 × 4 continuous bow (2339)

7) Arch 1 × 3 × 2 (88292)

8) Arch 1 × 3 × 2 inverted (18653)

9) Arch 1 × 3 × 3 (13965)

10) Arch 1 × 4 × 3 (80543)

11)   Arch 1 × 5 × 2 (3572)

12)   Arch 1 × 5 × 4 inverted (30099)

13)   Arch 1 × 4 (3659)

14)   Arch 1 × 4 × 2 (6182)

15)   Arch 1 × 6 raised arch (92950)

16)   Arch 1 × 6 × 2 medium thick top without reinforced underside (15254)

17)   Arch 1 × 6 × 2 curved top (6183)

18)   Arch 1 × 6 × 3 1/3 curved top (6060)

19)   Arch 1 × 8 × 2 (3308)

20)   Arch 1 × 12 × 3 raised arch with 5 cross supports (18838)

Slopes

As I have explained before, the simple application of slope pieces enabled LEGO creations to have a whole new dimension so it wasn't as 1 × 1 × 1 as Minecraft. Slopes come in all kinds of sizes to really create angles to your LEGO creation. You will note that there are numbers after the slope piece, which refers to the angle that it is, with the most common being 45. Slopes are great when it comes to creating a roof, and you can top them with a double-sloped piece.

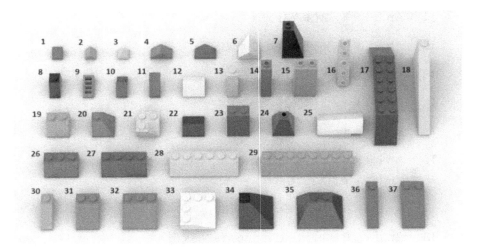

Figure 1-18. *Samples of slope LEGO pieces*

1) Slope 30 1 × 1 × 2/3 (54200)

2) Slope 45 1 × 1 double (35464)

3) Slope 45 1 × 1 × 2/3 quadruple convex pyramid (22388)

4) Slope 45 2 × 1 double with bottom stud holder (3044c)

5) Slope 45 2 × 1 triple with inside bar (3048c)

6) Slope 45 2 × 1 double/inverted (3049a)

7) Slope 75 2 × 2 × 3 double convex (3685)

8) Slope 45 2 × 1 (3040)

9) Slope 18 2 × 1 × 2/3 with grill (61409)

10) Slope 45 2 × 1 with 2/3 cutout (92946)

11) Slope 45 2 × 1 with cutout without stud (28192)

12)   Slope 45 2 × 2 double (3043)

13)   Slope 65 2 × 1 × 2 (60481)

14)   Slope 75 2 × 1 × 3 (4460b)

15)   Slope 75 2 × 2 × 3 (3684a)

16)   Slope 53 3 × 1 × 3 1/3 with studs on slope (6044)

17)   Slope 45 10 × 2 × 2 double (30180)

18)   Slope 25 8 × 1 × 3 (49618)

19)   Slope 45 2 × 2 (3039)

20)   Slope 45 2 × 2 double convex corner (3045)

21)   Slope 45 2 × 2 double concave (3046)

22)   Slope 33 2 × 2 double (3300)

23)   Slope 65 2 × 2 × 2 (3678b)

24)   Slope 75 2 × 2 × 2 quadruple convex (3688)

25)   Slope 45 2 × 4 × 1 1/3 double, tapered (80545)

26)   Slope 45 2 × 3 (3038)

27)   Slope 45 2 × 4 (3037)

28)   Slope 45 2 × 6 (23949)

29)   Slope 45 2 × 8 (4445)

30)   Slope 33 3 × 1 (4286)

31)   Slope 33 3 × 2(3298)

32)   Slope 33 3 × 3 (4161)

33)   Slope 33 3 × 3 double concave (99301)

34)   Slope 33 3 × 3 double convex corner (3675)

35)   Slope 45 3 × 4 double (4861)

36)   Slope 18 4 × 1 (60477)

37)   Slope 18 4 × 2 (30363)

Inverted Slopes

Some slopes start from the studs down, but an inverted slope goes
the other way. These are some examples of that, and they have a great
diversity.

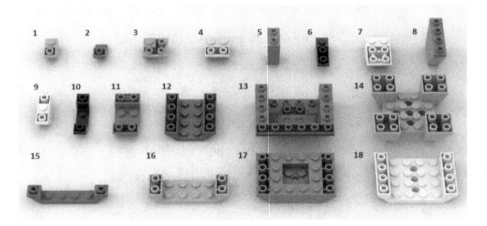

Figure 1-19. *Samples of LEGO inverted slopes*

1)   Slope inverted 45 2 × 1 (3665)

2)   Slope inverted 45 with 2/3 cutout (2310)

3)   Slope inverted 45 2 × 2 double convex (3676)

4)   Slope inverted 45 2 × 2 (3660)

5)   Slope inverted 75 2 × 1 × 3 (2449)

6)   Slope inverted 33 3 × 1 (4287)

7) Slope inverted 33 3 × 2 (3747b)

8) Slope inverted 60 4 × 1 × 3 (67440)

9) Slope inverted 45 3 × 1 double (2341)

10) Slope inverted 45 4 × 1 double (32802)

11) Slope inverted 45 4 × 2 double with 2 × 2 cutout (4871)

12) Slope inverted 45 4 × 4 double (4854)

13) Slope inverted 33 5 × 6 × 2 (4228)

14) Slope inverted 65 6 × 6 × 2 quad with cutouts (30373)

15) Slope inverted 45 6 × 1 double with 1 × 4 cutout (52501)

16) Slope inverted 45 6 × 2 double with 2 × 4 cutout (22889)

17) Slope inverted 45 6 × 4 double with recessed center (30183)

18) Slope inverted 45 6 × 4 double with 4 × 4 cutout and 3 holes (60219)

Slope Wedges

Not only can the slopes be inverted, they can slope to the sides as well, and this is a collection pieces that are capable of that. With the application of these wedge pieces, you can create shapes that are more than just square.

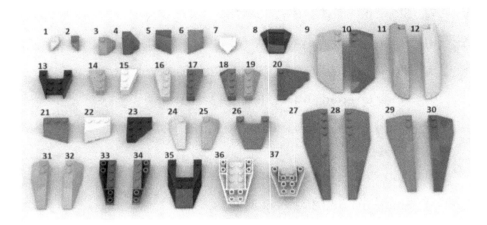

Figure 1-20. *Samples of slope wedges*

1) Wedge 2 × 1 × 2/3 left (29120)

2) Wedge 2 × 1 × 2/3 right (29119)

3) Wedge 2 × 2 slope 45 corner (13548)

4) Wedge 2 × 2 × 2 slope 65 corner (78886)

5) Wedge 3 × 2 right no studs (80178)

6) Wedge 3 × 2 left no studs (80177)

7) Wedge 2 × 2 × 2/3 pointed (66956)

8) Wedge 4 × 3 triple curved no studs (64225)

9) Wedge 8 × 3 × 2 open right (41749)

10) Wedge 8 × 3 × 2 open left (41750)

11) Wedge 10 × 2 × 2 right (77182)

12) Wedge 10 × 2 × 2 left (77180)

13) Wedge 3 1/2 × 4 with stud notches (50373)

14) Wedge 3 × 2 right (6564)

15) Wedge 3 × 2 left (6565)

16) Wedge 4 × 2 right (41767)

17) Wedge 4 × 2 left (41768)

18) Wedge 4 × 2 sloped right (43720)

19) Wedge 4 × 2 sloped left (43721)

20) Wedge 4 × 4 slope 18 corner (43708)

21) Wedge 3 × 3 sloped left (42862)

22) Wedge 3 × 3 sloped right (48165)

23) Wedge 3 × 3 facet (30505)

24) Wedge 4 × 2 triple right (43711)

25) Wedge 4 × 2 triple left (43710)

26) Wedge 4 × 4 taper without stud notches (4858)

27) Wedge 12 x 3 Right (42060)

28) Wedge 12 x 3 Left (42061)

29) Wedge 10 x 3 Right (50956)

30) Wedge 10 x 3 Left (50955)

31) Wedge 6 × 2 right (41747)

32) Wedge 6 × 2 left (41748)

33) Wedge 6 × 2 inverted right (41764)

34) Wedge 6 × 2 inverted left (41765)

35) Wedge 6 × 4 cutout with stud notches (6153b)

36) Wedge 6 × 4 triple inverted curved (43713)

37) Wedge 4 × 4 triple inverted with connections between 2 studs (4855)

Slope Curved

Just as the wedge pieces can create more than just square pieces, but more angular ones, you can also create some really curved creations with the help of the slope curved pieces.

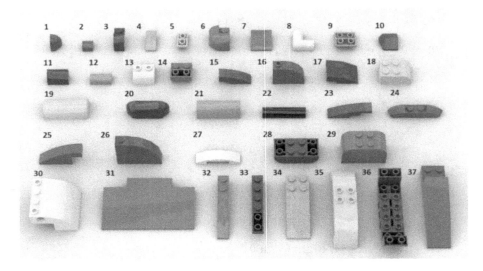

Figure 1-21. *Samples of LEGO slopes inverted*

1) Slope, curved 1 × 1 × 1 1/3 corner round (1871)

2) Slope, curved 1 × 1 × 2/3 double (49307)

3) Slope, curved 2 × 1 × 1 1/3 with recessed stud (6091)

4) Slope, curved 1 × 1 × 2/3 (11477)

5) Slope, curved 2 × 1 × 2/3 inverted (24201)

6) Slope, curved 2 × 2 × 1 1/3 corner round with recessed stud (67810)

7) Slope, curved 2 × 2 × 2/3 (15068)

8) Slope, curved 2 × 2 × 2/3 double corner (79757)

9) Slope, curved 2 × 2 × 2/3 inverted (32803)

10) Slope, curved 33 2 × 2 double inverted (1762)

11) Slope, curved 1 × 2 (37352)

12) Slope, curved 1 × 2 × 2/3 double (3563)

13) Slope, curved 2 × 2 double (30165)

14) Slope, curved 2 × 2 inverted (1750)

15) Slope, curved 3 × 1 (50950)

16) Slope, curved 3 × 1 × 2 with hollow stud (33243).

17) Slope, curved 3 × 2 (24309)

18) Slope, curved 3 × 2 with 4 studs (6215)

19) Slope, curved 2 × 4 double with groove stud (6192b)

20) Slope, curved 1 × 4 with rounded ends (4045).

21) Slope, curved 1 × 4 × 1 1/3 (6191)

22) Slope, curved 1 × 4 × 2/3 double (79756)

23) Slope, curved 4 × 1 (61678)

24) Slope, curved 4 × 1 double with 2 recessed
    studs (40996)

25) Slope, curved 4 × 1 × 1 2/3 (3573)

26) Slope, curved 4 × 1 × 2 2/3 with stud (65734)

27) Slope, curved 4 × 1 × 2/3 double (65734)

28) Slope, curved 4 × 2 inverted double (5174)

29) Slope, curved 4 × 2 × 2 double with 4 studs (4744)

30) Slope, curved 4 × 4 × 2 with 4 studs and peg
    holes (61487)

31)   Slope, curved 5 × 8 × 2/3 (71771)

32)   Slope, curved 6 × 1 (42022)

33)   Slope, curved 6 × 1 inverted (42023)

34)   Slope, curved 6 × 2 (44126)

35)   Slope, curved 8 × 2 × 2 (11290)

36)   Slope, curved 8 × 2 × 2 inverted double stud (11301)

37)   Slope, curved 8 × 2 × 2 with 4 recessed studs (41766)

Plates

The flat pieces of LEGO are known as plates, and they come in many forms. It takes a stack of three of the same area to equal one brick of the same volume. Creating a project with all blocks might make it look too blocky, for lack of a better word, but these pieces can give a lot more detailed definition to a creation.

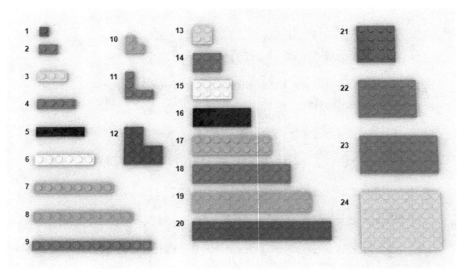

Figure 1-22. *Samples of LEGO plates*

1) Plate 1 × 1 (3024)

2) Plate 1 × 2 (3023)

3) Plate 1 × 3 (3623)

4) Plate 1 × 4 (3710)

5) Plate 1 × 5 (78329)

6) Plate 1 × 6 (3666)

7) Plate 1 × 8 (3460)

8) Plate 1 × 10 (4477)

9) Plate 1 × 12 (60479)

10) Plate 2 × 2 Corner (2420)

11) Plate 3 × 3 Corner (77844)

12) Plate 4 × 4 Corner (2639)

13) Plate 2 × 2 (3022)

14) Plate 2 × 3 (3021)

15) Plate 2 × 4 (3020)

16) Plate 2 × 6 (3795)

17) Plate 2 × 8 (3034)

18) Plate 2 × 10 (3832)

19) Plate 2 × 12 (2445)

20) Plate 2 × 14 (91988)

21) Plate 4 × 4 (3031)

22) Plate 4 × 6 (3032)

23) Plate 4 × 8 (3035)

24) Plate 6 × 8 (3036)

Plate Round

Just as the round bricks can make a creation more curvaceous, so can the plates. These are plates with round sections, made to give a less angular look.

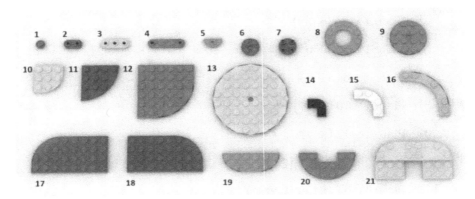

Figure 1-23. *Samples of round plate LEGO pieces*

1) Plate, round 1 × 1 (4073)

2) Plate, round 1 × 2 with open studs (35480)

3) Plate, round 1 × 3 with open studs (77850)

4) Plate, round 1 × 4 with 2 open studs (77845)

5) Plate, round 1 × 2 half with 1 stud (1745)

6) Plate, round 2 × 2 half with axle hole (4032)

7) Plate, round 2 × 2 with rounded bottom (2654)

8) Plate, round 4 × 4 with 2 × 2 round open center (11833)

9) Plate, round 4 × 4 with hole (60474)

10)   Plate, round corner 3 × 3 (30357)

11)   Plate, round corner 4 × 4 (30565)

12)   Plate, round corner 6 × 6 (6003)

13)   Plate, round 8 × 8 (74611)

14)   Plate, round corner 2 × 2 with 1 × 1 cutout (79491)

15)   Plate, round corner 3 × 3 with 2 × 2 curved cutout (68568)

16)   Plate, round corner 5 × 5 with 4 × 4 curved cutout (80015)

17)   Plate, round curved 4 × 8 left (712)

18)   Plate, round curved 4 × 8 right (713)

19)   Plate, round corner 2 × 6 double (18980)

20)   Plate, round half 3 × 6 with 1 × 2 cutout (18646)

21)   Plate, round 4 × 8 × 2/3, raised 2 × 8 and 2 × 2 cutout (73832)

Plate, Modified

Like the bricks, the plate can often have some extra involved, for adding interesting features to a creation with the modified plate.

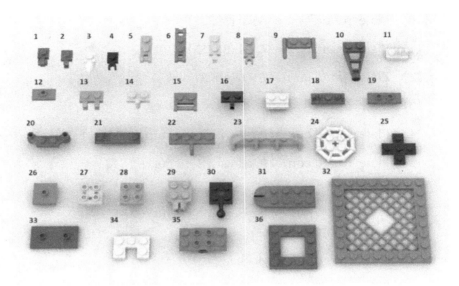

Figure 1-24. *Samples of modified plate LEGO pieces*

1) Plate, modified 1 × 1 with light attachment thick ring (4081b)

2) Plate, modified 1 × 1 with open O clip (61252)

3) Plate, modified 1 × 1 with tooth horizontal (49668)

4) Plate, modified 1 × 1 with U clip thick (4085c)

5) Plate, modified 1 × 2 with bar handle on end (60478)

6) Plate, modified 1 × 2 with bar handles on end (18649)

7) Plate, modified 1 × 2 with clip on end (63868)

8) Plate, modified 1 × 2 with bar handle on end (78256)

9) Plate, modified 1 × 2 with bar handles (3839a)

10) Plate, modified 1 × 2 with long stud holder (4596)

11) Plate, modified 1 × 2 with open O clip on top (44861)

12) Plate, modified 1 × 2 with 1 stud with groove (3794b)

13) Plate, modified 1 × 2 with open O clips (60470b)

14) Plate, modified 1 × 2 with bar arm up (4623b)

15) Plate, modified 1 × 2 with bar handle on side (48336)

16) Plate, modified 1 × 2 with clip on the side (11476)

17) Plate, modified 1 × 2 with door rail (32028)

18) Plate, modified 1 × 3 with 2 open O clips on top (79987)

19) Plate, modified 1 × 3 with 2 studs (34103)

20) Plate, modified 1 × 4 offset (4590)

21) Plate, modified 1 × 4 with 2 studs with groove (41740)

22) Plate, modified 1 × 4 with bar arm down (30043)

23) Plate, modified 1 × 6 with tan wagon end (4590)

24) Plate, modified 2 × 2 with bar frame octagonal (30033)

25) Plate, modified 3 × 3 cross (4590)

26) Plate, modified 2 × 2 with groove and 1 stud in Center (87580)

27) Plate, modified 2 × 2 with peg on bottom (2476b)

28) Plate, modified 2 × 2 with pegs on bottom (15092)

29) Plate, modified 2 × 2 with tow ball socket (3730)

30) Plate, modified 2 × 2 with tow ball and hole (15456)

31)   Plate, modified 2 × 5 with tow ball socket (3491)

32)   Plate, modified 8 × 8 with grill and 2 × 2 diamond cutout center (4151c)

33)   Plate, modified 2 × 4 with 2 studs (65509)

34)   Plate, modified 2 × 3 with 1 × 1 cutout (73831)

35)   Plate, modified 2 × 4 with peg holes (26599)

36)   Plate, modified 4 × 4 with 2 × 2 open center (64799)

Brackets

Sometimes, when you are building, you need to have some kind of 90 degree bend, to shift the studs from the top to the side. These would be the pieces that you would use.

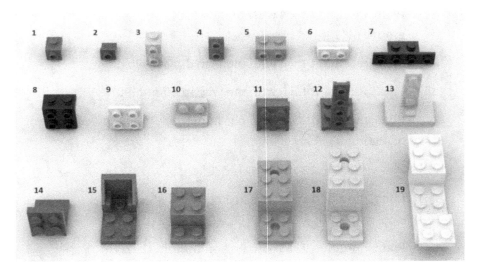

Figure 1-25. *Samples of LEGO brackets*

1) Bracket 1 × 1 – 1 × 1 (36841)

2) Bracket 1 × 1 – 1 × 1 inverted (36840)

3) Bracket 1 × 1 – 1 × 2 (79389)

4) Bracket 1 × 1 – 1 × 2 inverted (73825)

5) Bracket 1 × 1 – 1 × 2 (99781)

6) Bracket 1 × 2 – 1 × 2 inverted (99780)

7) Bracket 1 × 2 – 1 × 4 (2436)

8) Bracket 1 × 2 – 2 × 2 (44728)

9) Bracket 1 × 2 – 2 × 2 inverted (99207)

10) Bracket 2 × 2 – 1 × 2 centered (41682)

11) Bracket 2 × 2 – 2 × 2 with 2 holes (3956)

12) Bracket 2 × 2 – 1 × 4 (2422)

13) Bracket 2 × 3 – 1 × 3 (4169)

14) Bracket 2 × 2 – 2 × 2 (3956)

15) Bracket 3 × 2 – 2 × 2 inverted (4598)

16) Bracket 3 × 2 × 1 1/3 (18671)

17) Bracket 5 × 2 × 1 1/3 with 2 holes (11215)

18) Bracket 5 × 2 × 2 1/3 with 2 holes and bottom stud holder (76766)

19) Bracket 8 × 2 × 1 1/3 (4732)

Plate Wedge

I used to call these type of pieces wings, because this is what I primarily
used them for. When you need to have some product that needs to be wing
shaped, this is where this comes in handy.

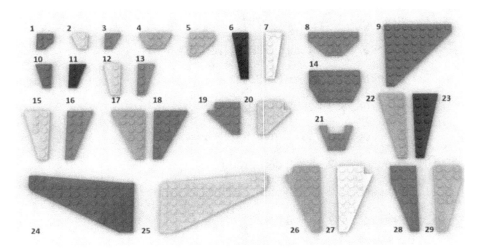

Figure 1-26. *Samples of plate wedge LEGO pieces*

1) Wedge, plate 2 × 2 cut corner (26601)

2) Wedge, plate 2 × 2 right (24307)

3) Wedge, plate 2 × 2 left (24299)

4) Wedge, plate 2 × 4 (51739)

5) Wedge, plate 3 × 3 cut corner (2450)

6) Wedge, plate 6 × 2 right (78444)

7) Wedge, plate 6 × 2 left (78443)

8) Wedge, plate 3 × 6 cut corners (2419)

9) Wedge, plate 8 × 8 cut corner (30504)

10)   Wedge, plate 3 × 2 right (43722)

11)   Wedge, plate 3 × 2 left (43723)

12)   Wedge, plate 4 × 2 right (41769)

13)   Wedge, plate 4 × 2 left (41770)

14)   Wedge, plate 4 × 6 cut corners (32059)

15)   Wedge, plate 6 × 3 right (54383)

16)   Wedge, plate 6 × 3 left (54384)

17)   Wedge, plate 6 × 4 right (48205)

18)   Wedge, plate 6 × 4 left (48208)

19)   Wedge, plate 4 × 4 wing right (3935)

20)   Wedge, plate 4 × 4 wing left (3935)

21)   Wedge, plate 3 × 4 without stud notches (4859)

22)   Wedge, plate 8 × 3 right (3545)

23)   Wedge, plate 8 × 3 left (3544)

24)   Wedge, plate 7 × 12 wing right (3585)

25)   Wedge, plate 7 × 12 left (3586)

26)   Wedge, plate 8 × 4 right without underside stud notch (3934a)

27)   Wedge, plate 8 × 4 left without underside stud notch (3933a)

28)   Wedge, plate 8 × 3 pentagonal right (50304)

29)   Wedge, plate 8 × 3 pentagonal left (50305)

Tiles

These plates have no studs on top and are good for when you want to literally smooth things over. This is really great when your creations have too much studs on them, and tile pieces cover the studs nicely.

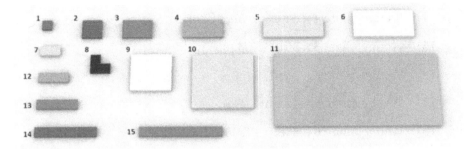

Figure 1-27. *Samples of LEGO tiles*

1)   Tile 1 × 1 (3070)

2)   Tile 2 × 2 (3068)

3)   Tile 2 × 3 (26603)

4)   Tile 2 × 4 (87079)

5)   Tile 2 × 6 (69729)

6)   Tile 3 × 6 (6934a)

7)   Tile 1 × 2 (3069)

8)   Tile 2 × 2 corner (14719)

9)   Tile 4 × 4 (1751)

10)   Tile 6 × 6 (6881)

11)   Tile 8 × 16 (48288)

12)   Tile 1 × 3 (63864)

13)   Tile 1 × 4 (2431)

14)   Tile 1 × 6 (6636)

15)   Tile 1 × 8 (4162)

Round Tiles

These tiles have a round look to them for more rounded creations that need to be smoothed over.

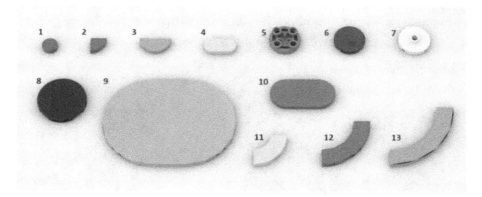

Figure 1-28. *Samples of LEGO round tiles*

1)   Tile, round 1 × 1 (98138)

2)   Tile, round 1 × 1 quarter (25269)

3)   Tile, round 1 × 2 half (1748)

4)   Tile, round 1 × 2 oval (1126)

5)   Tile, round 2 × 2 inverted (3567)

6)   Tile, round 2 × 2 (4150)

7)   Tile, round 2 × 2 with open stud (18674)

8)   Tile, round 3 × 3 (67095)

9)   Tile, round 6 × 8 oval (65474)

10)   Tile, round 2 × 4 oval (66857)

11)   Tile, round corner 2 × 2 macaroni (27925)

12)   Tile, round corner 3 × 3 macaroni (79393)

13)   Tile, round corner 4 × 4 macaroni wide (27507)

Modified Tiles

These are some great modified tiles for great purposes.

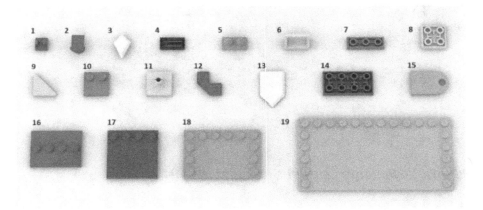

Figure 1-29. *Modified tiles in LEGO*

1)   Tile, modified 1 × 1 with clip (2555)

2)   Tile, modified 1 × 1 with tooth/ear vertical (35463)

3)   Tile, modified 1 × 2 diamond (35469)

4)   Tile, modified 1 × 2 grill with tooth/ear
     vertical (2412b)

5)   Tile, modified 1 × 2 with 2 teeth vertical (15209)

6)   Tile, modified 1 × 2 with bar handle (2432)

7)   Tile, modified 1 × 3 inverted with hole (35459)

8)   Tile, modified 2 × 2 inverted (11203)

9)   Tile, modified 2 × 2 triangular (35787)

10)   Tile, modified 2 × 2 with studs on edge (33909)

11)   Tile, modified 2 × 2 with peg (2460)

12)   Tile, modified facet 2 × 2 (27263)

13)   Tile, modified 1 × 3 pentagonal (22385)

14)   Tile, modified 2 × 4 inverted (3395)

15)   Tile, modified 3 × 2 with hole (48995)

16)   Tile, modified 3 × 4 with 4 studs in the center (88646)

17)   Tile, modified 4 × 4 with 4 studs on edge (6179)

18)   Tile, modified 4 × 6 with studs on edges (6180)

19)   Tile, modified 6 × 12 with studs on edges (6178)

Hinges

As the name implies, hinges are when you have a section that you want to move around deliberately, or stay frozen. That, or stay frozen at an angle that is not 90 degrees.

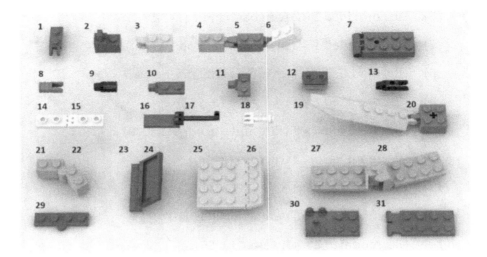

Figure 1-30. *Samples of LEGO hinge pieces*

1) Hinge plate 1 × 2 locking with 2 fingers on end (44302a)

2) Hinge brick 1 × 2 locking with 1 finger top (989)

3) Hinge brick 1 × 2 locking with 2 fingers (54672)

4) Hinge brick 1 × 2 locking with 1 finger horizontal end (30541)

5) Hinge brick 1 × 2 locking with 1 finger vertical end (47975)

6) Hinge brick 1 × 2 locking with 2 fingers vertical end (54671)

7) Hinge plate 2 × 4 (3149c01)

8) Hinge cylinder 1 × 2 locking with 2 fingers and axle hole (57360)

9) Hinge cylinder 1 × 2 locking with 1 finger and axle hole (53923)

10) Hinge plate 1 × 2 locking with 1 finger on end with bottom groove (44301a)

11) Hinge plate 1 × 2 locking with 1 finger on side with bottom groove (44567a)

12) Hinge brick 1 × 2 top plate and base (3937 and 3938)

13) Hinge cylinder 1 × 3 locking with 1 finger and 2 fingers on ends (54662)

14) Hinge plate 1 × 2 with 2 fingers (4276b)

15) Hinge plate 1 × 2 with 3 fingers on end (4275b)

16) Hinge tile 1 × 2 with 2 fingers on top (4531)

17) Hinge bar 2.5 M with 2 and 3 fingers on ends (2880)

18) Hinge bar with 3 fingers and end stud (2433)

19) Hinge plate 1 × 8 with angled side (30407)

20) Hinge brick 2 × 2 locking with 1 finger vertical and axle hole (30389b)

21) Hinge brick 1 × 4 swivel base (3831)

22) Hinge brick 1 × 4 swivel top (3830)

23) Hinge tile 1 × 4 (4625)

24) Hinge train gate 2 × 4 (2873)

25) Hinge vehicle roof 4 × 4 (4213)

26) Hinge plate 1 × 4 (4315)

27) Hinge plate 2 × 4 with articulated joint male (3639)

28) Hinge plate 2 × 4 with articulated joint female (3640)

29) Hinge plate 1 × 4 swivel (2429c01)

30)   Hinge plate 2 × 4 female (3597)

31)   Hinge plate 2 × 4 male (3315)

A Word About Technic

In case you are wondering why I haven't talked about Technic pieces yet, it is because I have another book that is devoted to creating with LEGO Technic.

I have to admit that these Technic bricks, which were the basic units of building in the old Technic kits, have phased out these bricks for the beams, which I will discuss right now. I did want to bring them up because they can be used, but there won't be much talked about here.

You might note how the studs are hollowed out on top, but not certain why that is. The important thing is the sides of Technic bricks allow the access of axles and connector pegs, which I won't discuss at all in this book. However, I brought up a few modified bricks that work well with these Technic pieces.

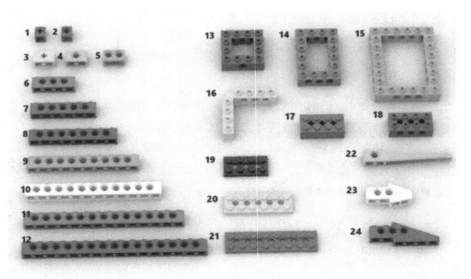

Figure 1-31. *Samples of LEGO Technic bricks*

1. Technic brick 1 × 1 with axle hole (73230): A typical
    1 × 1 brick with an axle hole in the middle

2. Technic brick 1 × 1 with hole (6541): Another typical
    1 × 1 brick with a Technic addition of a through hole.
    Generally, the number of through holes is equal
    to the number of studs, minus one, but this is one
    exception

3. Technic brick 1 × 2 with axle hole (32064): A 1 × 2
    brick with an axle hole

4. Technic brick 1 × 2 with hole (3700): Typical round
    hole in a 1 × 2 typical brick

5. Technic brick 1 × 2 with holes (32000): Another
    exception to the number of through holes equal to
    the number of studs, minus one

6. Technic brick 1 × 4 with holes (3701): With one
    exception, LEGO Technic bricks generally have an
    even number of studs, and this is one of the smallest
    at a length of 4 M with three round holes on the side.
    The rest of Technic bricks increase by 2 M or two
    studs, and the rule of the number of round holes on
    the side is equal to the number of studs, minus one

7. Technic brick 1 × 6 with holes (3894)

8. Technic brick 1 × 8 with holes (3702)

9. Technic brick 1 × 10 with holes (2730)

10. Technic brick 1 × 12 with holes (3895)

11. Technic brick 1 × 14 with holes (32018)

12. Technic brick 1 × 16 with holes (3703)

13. Technic brick 4 × 4 open center (32324): Of course, it is possible to create this piece with several other Technic brick pieces, but it is good to start a creation with a solid form such as this

14. Technic brick 4 × 6 open center (32531)

15. Technic brick 6 × 8 open center (32532)

16. Technic brick 5 × 5 right angle (32555): Like traditional LEGO bricks, LEGO Technic bricks come with corner pieces

17. Technic brick 2 × 4 with 3 axle holes (39789): This is a typical 2 × 4 brick with 3 axle holes in the middle

18. Technic brick 2 × 4 with holes on all sides (3709a): A typical 2 × 4 brick with through holes on the sides and top

19. Technic plate 2 × 4 with 3 holes (3709b): Like the brick, the LEGO plate also had through holes, equal to the number of pieces in the length, minus one

20. Technic plate 2 × 6 with 5 holes (32001)

21. Technic plate 2 × 8 with 7 holes (3738)

22. Technic forklift fork (2823): This is essentially a 1 × 2 Technic brick with an odd extension that takes it to a length of 6 M. I believe it is called a fork as it used to be used in LEGO sets with forklifts

23. Technic slope 4 × 1 × 2 1/3 (2743): LEGO Technic used to have sets with airplanes that had these types of LEGO bricks, before moving to beams

24. Technic slope 6 × 1 × 1 2/3 (2744)

I also mentioned in that video that LEGO Technic pieces are starting to be used in more traditional LEGO sets. So if you are a collector of the more traditional sets, that is for you.

This is just a brief introduction to LEGO pieces, but it is by no means an exhaustive list. I'm sure that if I had to list out every type of piece that LEGO has produced in the past few decades of the company's creation, it would fill several books.

There will be some types of pieces that I will highlight in later chapters, but for now, you should organize your LEGO piece collection so that they are in these categories. This way, it makes it easy to find, even if you might have to sift through these subsets to find the exact piece you are looking for.

So now that you have all these pieces, and they are organized, now what? First of all, I think it is about time we got more into detail, so let's conclude this chapter.

Conclusion

No matter what you build, you are going to need an idea of where to begin. Chances are you already know what you want to build, but it might seem so large that you don't know have absolutely no idea of where to begin.

One of the reasons why I went through so much LEGO history is that I wanted to really spotlight how LEGO has changed throughout the years, and looking at older or newer sets is a great way to get ideas for what and even how to build certain things. It is one of the things that really helped me write this book.

If you need more pieces, it is relatively easy to find bundles of bricks available on many online auctions at cheap prices. If you are just looking for lots of pieces, you will probably find a general collection that you can purchase for a low price. When it comes to finding individual sets and pieces, that when it might get costly.

You probably have a lot of LEGO sets from times past, and it just makes sense to sort out all the pieces before you start building. Of course, if you are going to build, then you are going to need a plan. Also, if you want to build big, which I highly recommend, you should start a base for that, and these are subjects that we will cover in the next chapter.

CHAPTER 2

Planning in LEGO Virtually with Architecture: The Model Before the Model

Okay, now that you have all your pieces, it is time to get to building. Of course, you might want to ask yourself if you can even do what you want. I would suggest that you take the time to plan it out.

In Chapter 1, I mentioned how I had a friend who built a mothership that was 4 feet long and how this inspired me to build with LEGO again, but at the time, I only had a few Universal Building Kits, a Classic Space LEGO set, and a few others.

There was no way that I could have built something so massive, but I certainly wish that I had some kind of software that could plan out building projects. Fortunately, this technology exists today, and the best part about it is that you don't have to worry if you have enough pieces, because you can virtually call up any piece that you need, in any color that you want.

© Mark Rollins 2024
M. Rollins, *Ultimate LEGO Worldbuilding and Architecture*, Maker Innovations Series,
https://doi.org/10.1007/979-8-8688-0521-9_2

That is just one topic that we will cover in this chapter, because not
only are we going to talk about building in a virtual world with third-party
software made for making anything in LEGO, but we need to discuss how
to make a strong LEGO base for your LEGO creation.

Building with LEGO in a Virtual World

By now, you have hopefully been able to assemble the basics of a Technic kit.
By that, I mean a good collection of pieces that I discussed in Chapter 1. Yet
even if you can't find any pieces anywhere, there is a place where you could
find any piece of any kind, in any color you want.

Fortunately, this technology exists today, and it is absolutely free.
Granted, you might not be able to hold a piece in your hand, nor your
model, but you will be able to see what it looks like. Not only that, you will
be able to see if it is even possible to build it as the program figures out if
the LEGO pieces exist in that color and even check to see if the structure
is stable.

Stud.io

I highly recommend downloading the latest version of Stud.io. I had a bit
of an issue when I downloaded it for the first time, so I recommend that
you find the latest version, which you can find on BrickLink here: `www.`
`bricklink.com/v3/studio/download.page`. From the very beginning,
there is a great tutorial where you had to build a snail, and it was enough to
show how to select a piece and then manipulate it in real time.

The advantage of Stud.io is that you can select a piece from many
categories, and I designed the categories of LEGO pieces in Chapter 1
of this book to correspond to the categories on Stud.io. Underneath that
section, you can search the parts for what piece you need, but I had to
admit that unless you actually know the official name or number, you

might have better results doing a visual search. For example, the arch
pieces are found under the Bricks Modified section, which is the last place
I would have instinctively looked for them.

I have to admit that I really like the interface of Stud.io. I have used
other LEGO drawing programs like LDraw and LeoCAD for my other
LEGO books, and I found them to be somewhat taxing. Stud.io reminds me
a lot of Lego Digital Designer, which is a program that LEGO used to have
available where you just select a brick and set it in 3D space. If you know
how to navigate the Top, Left, and Right Menus, then you will quickly learn
how to build faster as you access all the features of Stud.io.

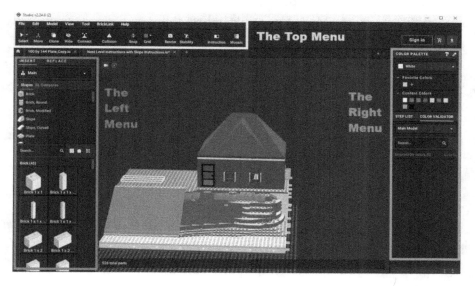

Figure 2-1. *Screenshot of Stud.io, but I highlighted the Left, Right,
and Top Menus*

The Left Menu

You will notice that once a LEGO piece is selected, you can use the arrow keys to determine its direction and position, and it will flip it or turn it at 90 degrees. If you want to do some other angle, you can select the rotation tool, and that will allow you to turn it at a very precise angle, and I have demonstrations of this in this chapter and others.

While I'm on the subject of manipulating a piece, you can also click on the Move tool, which will allow you to move a brick in a limited space in the x-axis, y-axis, or z-axis. You can use this tool in places where the Stud.io AI won't allow you to put a brick in a certain place. Or at least not without great difficulty, so the Move tool really helps limit the LEGO piece mobility so you can get it in place.

You will notice that you can select "Replace," which is a handy tool to use while you are building. You will have to select the brick that you are working on, and it will only suggest bricks that take up the same basic shape. For example, if you select a 2 × 4 brick, it will give you suggestions that include a 2 × 4 plate, 2 × 4 slope, or any other brick that takes up the same area, but not necessarily the same volume.

There is also a button here that can change all the LEGO pieces to a certain color, and you can see that LEGO pieces come in all the colors of the rainbow and much more. In fact, it is quite possible that LEGO does not even make a certain shape in a certain color, something you will need to think about if you want to bring your creation to life. This would be a good time for me to say that I use some bricks with colors that LEGO does not make as illustrations in this book, at least in Chapter 1. As I said in Chapter 1, there are times where I change the color of a particular brick for emphasis, but for the most part, most of the models in this book can be built in real life with the colors that LEGO offers you.

There is also an option for toggling Decorated Bricks on and off. Decorated Bricks is exactly what it sounds like, a LEGO piece that has some kind of permanent writing or picture. I didn't cover Decorated Bricks at all in Chapter 1 because I wanted to discuss pieces in their most blank form, but LEGO, with its thousands of sets throughout the past decades, has had quite many Decorated Bricks. I'm very certain the last chapter would have been multiplied greatly if I included every Decorated Brick that LEGO has created. As an added note, Decorated Bricks are different from the stickers that LEGO has in some of their sets, which I don't think are really possible to apply with Stud.io.

There is another button here that will change the layout of the piece menu so you can see what you have work with in a column that is 1, 2, or 3 pieces wide. I have to admit that I had some issues with this, because the smaller a piece is on the screen, the harder it is to recognize.

The Right Menu

The default menu on the right is set up for the colors of the piece, and a way to color any piece selected with whatever color that you want. Like I said before, you can color a piece with a color that LEGO doesn't make in Stud.io. You will notice that pieces of a certain color will have exclamation marks on them, which means that you won't be able to find a piece of that shape available in that color. I don't suggest using a piece that is not available in that color, and there is a way to make a correction on this if you like using the Color Validator.

The Color Validator is a terrific tool that allows for some easy editing in case you have a piece that is in a color that LEGO does not produce. You can even have Stud.io do an autocorrect on it to give it a color that LEGO does have of its type. For example, I had a brick modified 2 × 4 × 2 with holes on sides that was in purple, but the Color Validator noted that the piece is available in black and made the correction.

This menu also has a place to set up steps. Think of it as steps in a LEGO instruction booklet, and it comes in handy when you are creating any project from the ground up. Of course, you can always create something from the ground down, like you can create a roof and work your way down to build the house underneath it. After all, you are not limited by gravity in a 3D virtual world.

If you want to create instructions for yourself, like the ones that I have
in my books, I highly recommend using the step tool. The issue is that you
need to be conscious of it, because the Step List will only record whatever
steps that you use as you select your pieces.

So as you build, hit "Add Step", and this will create a place for the
pieces you will use, and then keep going. You can right click each step
and move the pieces around, delete them, or even hide them, which I will
explain later.

The Top Menu

Like most programs, your basic needs can be met on the menu on top,
and we'll start with the visible tiles. Select allows you to highlight a certain
piece, and hitting CTRL will highlight multiple pieces. From there, you can
use the Rotation and Move tool and other options.

You can also select a piece by color, like if you want to select all the blue
bricks, you can do that, and you can do whatever you want with them. You
can even select a piece by type and color, not to mention by Connection.

Hinge allows you to select a piece and then change the specific angle
on it. It can be manipulated in three dimensions, and this is how you can
make hinge pieces work for you. We briefly discussed in Chapter 1 how
the hinge pieces work and Stud.io allows you to adjust the angles of them
in its virtual space.

The Clone allows a piece to be immediately duplicated, and a copy of
the piece will appear directly atop of the piece selected. It is a great way to
build up walls, but not a way to make walls architecturally strong, and I will
explain that later.

Hide will hide a piece. The reason you would want to do that is because
there are times where you will want to put a piece somewhere, but the AI
doesn't know how to process it. So you can try dragging it to a spot, and
it won't go where you want it to. It helps to hide pieces around that piece,
and you will have an easier time putting it in place. By the way, if a piece is

hidden, Stud.io will show the number of hidden pieces on the screen, and it is possible to reveal them all at the touch of button.

Connect is an excellent tool for just linking bricks. There are going to be times where the AI can't figure out what you are trying to do with a certain brick, like if you can't fit one in where it needs to go. For this, I recommend just clicking the place where you want the first brick and then clicking where it needs to go.

There is also a Collision button that, when engaged, will allow you to see if parts will fit together. Stud.io will often allow you to put pieces in places where they would not regularly fit, which can be problematic if you are trying to build a real-life model.

The Snap button is usually defaulted to "On", and you will discover that when it is off, the piece will go literally wherever. However, with the Snap mode engaged, pieces will drag and then stick where they need to.

For the Grid function, this will regulate how far a piece will move with the directional controls. You can move it one stud at a time, or with smaller movements. By the way, you can move a selected piece with the W, A, S, and D keys.

Render is where you can take your creation and really put it in a great image. You will find that a lot of the illustrations in this book have been created with Render, and I am surprised at the photo-realism that is possible. It will take time to render that image, and the more realistic you want, the longer it will take.

Stability is where you will start to get a warning about how safe is your creation. Anything that looks very questionable is taken into account, and it will warn you by highlighting it in red. I highly recommend using this while you are building, because Stud.io will be able to find weak points in your construction and highlight them accordingly.

Instruction will take your steps and put them in a form like a traditional LEGO set of instructions. As I mentioned before, you have to highlight what is a step as you are building, which can be very difficult because most of us don't think about how to do instructions as we are building.

Mosaic is an interesting tool that allows you to upload an image and
then make it so it is a mosaic, which is a really fantastic tool that we won't
really cover in this book. We're going to focus more on creating LEGO
worlds on a minifig scakle.

The LEGO City

All right, let's say that you have figured out what it is that you want to
build. Of course, I am going to recommend that you build it in Stud.io first,
because it is most certainly a tool that has helped me. As for me, I decided
to build a small LEGO City, by showing you some really cool techniques,
and then, you can put variations of your own on it.

Even though Stud.io allows me to build on a space that is virtually
infinite, reality is somewhat more limited. Therefore, I recommend that
you plan your real-world space. Now, if you are building something that
is relatively small, like 9.5 in^2, there is a LEGO baseplate for that. In fact,
LEGO makes several of these.

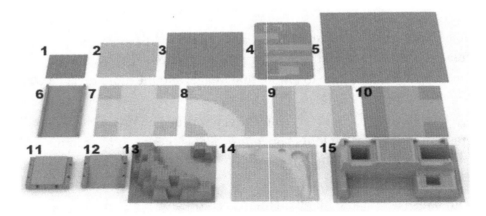

Figure 2-2. *A selection of LEGO baseplates*

1) Baseplate 16 × 16 (3867)

2) Baseplate 24 × 24 (367a)

3) Baseplate 32 × 32 (3811)

4) Baseplate 24 × 40 with gravel quarry sets 360/580 dots pattern (809)

5) Baseplate 50 × 50 (4186a)

6) Baseplate, road 32 × 16 ramp, Straight (30401)

7) Baseplate, road 32 × 32 9-stud crossroads (607)

8) Baseplate, road 32 × 32 9-stud curve (609)

9) Baseplate, road 32 × 32 9-stud straight (606)

10) Baseplate, road 32 × 32 9-stud T-intersection no pattern (608)

11) Baseplate, raised platform 16 × 16 × 2 1/3 (2617)

12) Baseplate, raised platform 16 × 16 × 2 1/3 ramp (2642)

13) Baseplate, raised 32 × 32 canyon (6024)

14) Baseplate, raised 32 × 32 crater plate without crater studs (3947a)

15) Baseplate, raised 32 × 48 × 6 with level front (51542)

The LEGO baseplate is really good for when you just want to create that foundation, but when you turn them on their side, you will find that your foundation is almost paper thin in some cases. Also, those baseplates that are not so flat, but have details such as craters and rocks, which might work against you, depending on your project. I am going to recommend that if you want to build larger, then create something that is bigger and thicker and will be very sturdy.

I have a table that I want to build my city on, and it is 29 inches wide
and 46 inches long. I was trying to figure out how wide and long I have, in
terms of studs. I took out a 6 × 12 plate and measured it, and it was a little
under 2 ×4 inches. Since I wanted something a little more exact that I could
work with, I decided to Google the measurement of a 1 × 1 brick, to find it
to be about 5/16 of an inch, which translates in metric at about 7.9375 mm
or 8 mm.

So, if I divide 29 by 5/16, I get 92.8, which is how wide my creation can
be in terms of LEGO studs. I could round that up to 93, but I would prefer
rounding down to 92, as I would prefer to have some room to work here. If
my creation goes past the edge of the table, even a little, that could cause
problems later on, so I would prefer it to stay within the confines.

As far as the length is concerned, I can do the same calculation with 46
divided by 5/16, obtaining a value of 147.2. I suppose that I could round
this up to 148, but perhaps I should keep it at 146, because I've discovered
that when building with LEGO, things work better with even numbers.

Speaking of even numbers, I was really hoping that this final
calculation of 92 × 146 would work better as far as something that would
be divisible by four. Looks like it didn't end up that way, did it? I'm going
to bring it down to 80 × 144, as I can lay out a base much easier using those
figures. After all, 144 is easily divisible by 12, and this is going to work a
whole lot better for us.

After I did this, I had a change of mind. I decided to do 100 × 144.
Granted, I would need a bigger table, but I do have one. I figure that it
would be easy do some kind of base if I used a width and length that are
perfect squares (a number that is a product of two equal integers).

For now, I want to figure out what I can do with this. I am going to use
principles in LEGO Architecture.

LEGO Architecture

My next few chapters are going to be about building buildings. So, I'm
going to need to set up a plan of what I want to do from there.

I'm going to use the power of LEGO Architecture, and if you aren't
familiar with that, it is a really great series. The sets that I have seen are too
small for minifig scale, as in many cases, your minifigs would have to be
smaller than the size of a 1 × 1 plate to accommodate these structures. For
example, some of the structures, such as the pyramids and the Louvre are
very large, and the LEGO Architecture cityscapes are quite grand. To put a
minifig on one of these sets would make them a giant in that type of realm.

Figure 2-3. *Samples of LEGO Architecture sets from LEGO. Take note
of the scale*

So, I am going to scale this down, quite a bit. Since I have this set up at
100 × 144, I'm going to pretend that I have shrunk it to a 8 × 14 plate. Yes,
that leaves a little bit to spare on the width wise, but it translates to about
one stud equal to ten studs. Yes, I made the width a little smaller, but at this
point, you don't need to be too accurate.

I mentioned that I wanted to create a LEGO town, and this is where the
big picture comes in. Since land is rarely flat, I have decided to raise up a
section of it using sloped bricks. I then fill in the rest with bricks to make
up the next level of the town. Just for the sake of scale, I gave it a nice tan
coating.

71

All right, the first thing that I am going to do is plan a road to go
through the town, and I'm going to just lay one out using tiles, not to
mention the slopes.

You will notice that in the scale model, my roads are about 20 studs
wide, which accounts for two lanes with traffic flowing in either direction
measured at 10 studs each. You might think that that is a lot of space to
devote to the roads, but lanes are about 9 to 15 feet wide in reality, so we
will have to make our LEGO vehicles comparable. As far as how I am going
to make the roads work with the downward slopes, that is another issue I
will have to tackle, but I'm saving that for the next chapter.

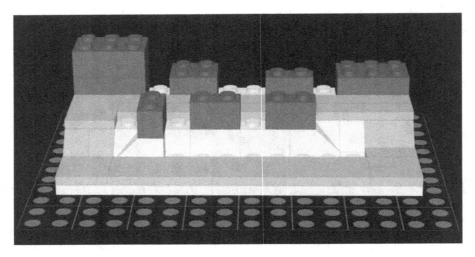

Figure 2-4. *A very small model of what I intend to build*

So, now the question remains as far as what buildings are put there.
Since the roads take up a lot of room, I'm going to have to put the buildings
in such a way that it works out well.

Now, I haven't even really decided what these buildings are for. I
suppose they could be houses or businesses, and I made one two-story tall
just for variety. I'm probably going to make them taller, but there is a limit
to what I can do, honestly. Buildings made too high have to be secured or
they could topple over under their own weight.

Speaking of limits, I also have to account for parking in this city, right? I might be able to turn the bottom floors of one of things buildings into a place for parking, and I have to account on spaces between the vehicles.

There is also things to be accounted for when it comes to spaces, because, if these buildings are houses, no one has a backyard, not to mention any room for a front yard. If I want to make this work, I might need more space, or at least a bigger table.

These are the questions that you also have to account for when dealing with this. So now, it is time to ask yourself a few questions.

What Is It That You Want to Build?

Do you want to make some LEGO diorama of a cityscape, or some setting from a movie or book? Whether this is based on something real or something from your imagination, you don't necessarily have to plan every single detail. After all, you're going to discover that you can have some room to make quick changes.

How Much Space Do You Have to Work With?

Like I did before, I found the table that I wanted to build my project on. I have seen huge LEGO creations that fill up a room, and even though I have no idea if they started that way, they certainly need a place to stay. I definitely recommend measuring the area that you are going to work with and then doing a conversion to studs (inches divided by 5/16) to see what you can work with.

From there, you are then going to have to look at all your plates to see if you can have a good surface to start with. I'm going to talk about what to do when that happens.

Should You Make a Smaller Scale Model First?

I will leave it up to you if you want to answer this question, but I
recommend that you look at the big picture first. For example, if you
want to make some kind of city, like I did, then you should at least plan
out the roads and other types of basic requirements before looking
into the infrastructure. For me, I like to think about every minifig in the
construction and making certain that they can live in the LEGO creation
just like I live in my own town. I'm not saying that you have to create
bathrooms or other sort of LEGO structures, but anything that you can
build in your LEGO creation to bring it to life really helps out a lot.

Creating a 100 × 144 LEGO Base

Okay, so this is going to be as simple LEGO construction as it gets.
In the end, you are going to get a slab that you can build a very large
creation upon. It might seem basic, and it is, but it demonstrates how to
build strong.

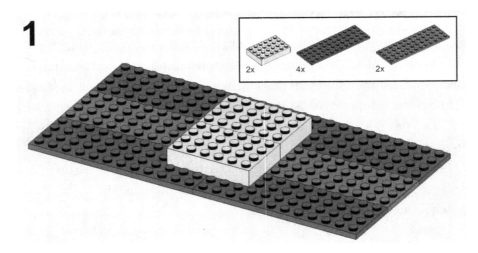

Figure 2-5. *Once you have the 4 × 12 plates, connect them together
with the 4 × 6 bricks*

For the first step, I alternated the colors so it would be easily visible. Speaking of colors, most of the LEGO pieces of this are not going to be visible in steps 1–8, so I didn't really focus on that.

The important thing about building this base is making sure that you apply what I call the two-stud overlap, which will allow these LEGO pieces to really stay together.

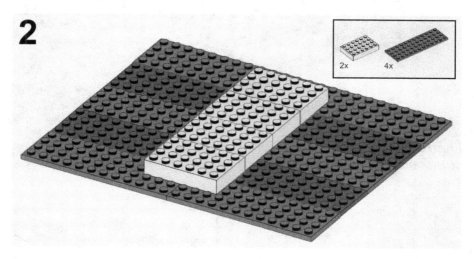

Figure 2-6. *Put on two more 4 × 6 bricks, and then add on the 4 × 12 plates*

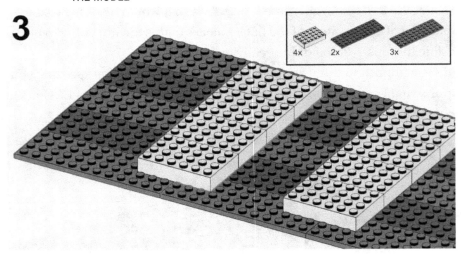

Figure 2-7. *Add on the 4 × 6 bricks, and then add on the 4 × 12
plates, which will widen the creation quite a bit*

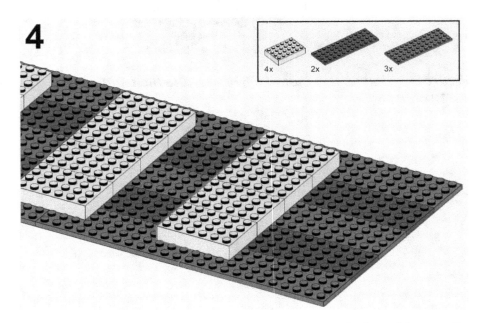

Figure 2-8. *Time to widen the base even more with the addition of
more 4 × 6 bricks and 4 × 12*

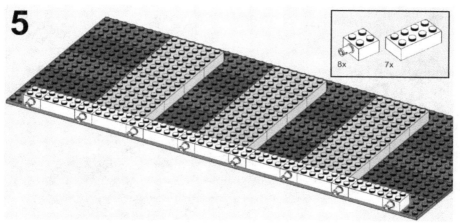

Figure 2-9. *Time to do the side with the brick, modified 2 × 2 with peg, as well as the 2 × 4 bricks*

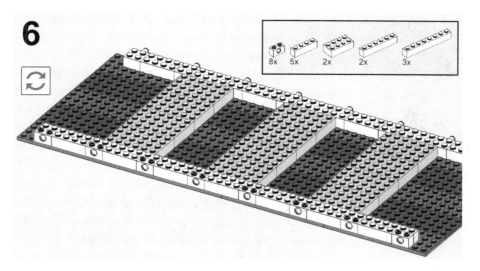

Figure 2-10. *Turn the creation around, and put on the 2 × 4, 1 × 6, and 1 × 8 bricks. Then, it is time to put on the 1 × 4 bricks, with the 1 × 2 bricks with hole*

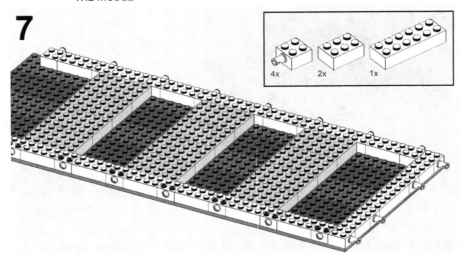

Figure 2-11. *Focus on the right side with the brick modified 2 × 2
with connector peg, and then put on the 2 × 3 and 2 × 6 bricks*

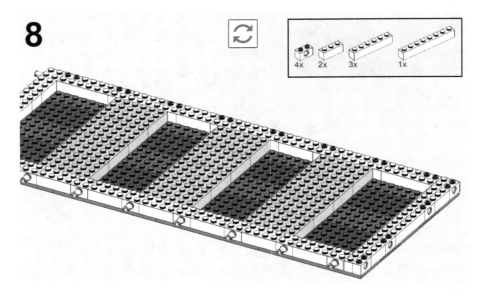

Figure 2-12. *Turn around the creation and put on the 1 × 6 and 1 × 8
bricks. Put on the 1 × 2 bricks with hole with the 1 × 3 bricks*

9

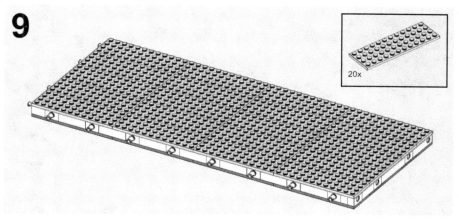

20x

Figure 2-13. *Time to cap off the creation with many 4 × 12 plates*

Now that you have this 20 × 48 plate, you can essentially create more of
them to create an even larger surface to put your LEGO creation on. This is
why those modified bricks are on the sides.

So, if you create two more of these 20 × 48 plates, you can attach one
on the right and one on the left to create a surface that is 20 × 144 studs in
its area.

Figure 2-14. *Attaching three sections of the 20 × 48 base to create a
superstrong base of 20 × 144*

From there, you can make two more 20 × 144 sections and put one on
the top (or north side) and another at the bottom (or south side), and you
have a section that is 60 × 144.

Figure 2-15. *A 60 × 144 base, made by linking three sections of the
20 × 144 together*

Then, all you need to do is add on two more 20 × 144 sections, and you
will have a 100 × 144 stud platform.

Figure 2-16. *The 100 × 144 base, made up of 15 sections of the
20 × 48 base linked together*

Not only is it designed to take a lot of weight and serve as a foundation
for your LEGO creation, but this can be easily taken apart into smaller
pieces. This will come in handy in case you want to move this anywhere.
Granted, you might have to build your creation so it can be easily removed,
or break apart in between the seams of the base.

Conclusion

For those who want to "go big or go home," this is where you want to plan it
out. I recommend downloading Stud.io and get familiar with how it works.

Once you have figured out what you want to build, it might be a good
idea to create a small-scale version of what you want to build using the
principles of LEGO Architecture. That is, figure out the scale you want to
do just so you can see a big picture.

From there, it is time to create a base for your creation. It will involve a
lot of plates and bricks, and they need to be linked together with a two-
stud overlap. Your base can be as large as your number of pieces can allow,
and it can be a great place to start.

However, your creation is might seem boring if it is just two
dimensional on a flat land, so it is time to take it to the next level, which
leads to the next chapter.

CHAPTER 3

How to Build a Strong LEGO Base That Is Ready for Expansion

Okay, at this point, you might be reading this book and thinking: what the heck, I want to build some huge LEGO diorama from my favorite franchise, and this guy spends an entire chapter on making a huge slab?

Yes, that was Chapter 2, and I did it to illustrate the need to have a solid foundation when you are creating some kind of LEGO creation of any kind. Not only that, I wanted to illustrate the points of building strong and how it is good to follow the "two-stud overlap" rule when creating something in LEGO so it will stand strong. Oh, and you should really use Stud.io or some other 3D building program in virtual LEGO.

Speaking of 3D, it should be known that you don't want to build your creations with a foundation that is flat, and this is how to take them to the next level.

The Reality of Ground Level

This next chapter might seem to be also on the long side, and it illustrates how to create a next level to your foundation. Like I said in the last chapter, you can make your base as long as wide as you want it, but here's the deal: flat is boring.

© Mark Rollins 2024
M. Rollins, *Ultimate LEGO Worldbuilding and Architecture*, Maker Innovations Series,
https://doi.org/10.1007/979-8-8688-0521-9_3

So yes, you can skip ahead to the next chapters that will give you advice on how to make houses and vehicles and other things that will really bring your creation to life. However, if you want to make your creation as lifelike as possible, then you should know that, contrary to what a (hopefully) small minority may say, the Earth is not flat.

Even in your own neighborhood, the roads that are straight and narrow have been made that way using a lot of time and construction equipment. Even with all that work, steep hills still exist in constructed streets. Things that are flat are often not in nature, and since you are going to build something that is supposed to resemble something from this world, you might as well make it as real as it can be.

So part of this is going to be how to make a landscape, and I decided to show it using a kind of split-level sort of view. You can see the very small diorama that I made in Chapter 2 and how I want to have some buildings on a second level, with a road that goes through them, and this road slopes downward into a lower level. Consider that a sneak preview, and like most builders, I have to figure out how to make that dream, and small model of that dream, into a reality.

Now, I could have made this upper level a solid thick slab of bricks, but I figured that I would save a little on bricks. After all, there is no reason to make something solid brick unless it needs to be, and I actually gave some room for growth by creating a hollow area underneath the city section. Of course, you could use Duplo bricks to create something solid and put LEGO bricks over those, but I won't go into detail about that in this book.

I will show you that if you go to another level, then it has to be architecturally sound, which means you got to make strong pillars to hold the weight above it. You don't want your next level to literally fall to pieces because of the weight, so I will show how to make something that should hold what you want it to hold.

Creating a Next Level to Your Solid Base

For this next particular model, we are going to go back to the 20 × 48 plate, and we're going to make it so it has a "second story" to it. So, yes, you will need to build one of these bases to do this next level.

Keep in mind that you can make these pillars even more stable by making them thicker or putting more supports on top. So without further ado, here's how to make a next level.

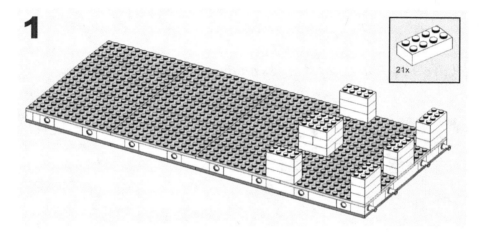

Figure 3-1. *Put on the 2 × 4 bricks as shown*

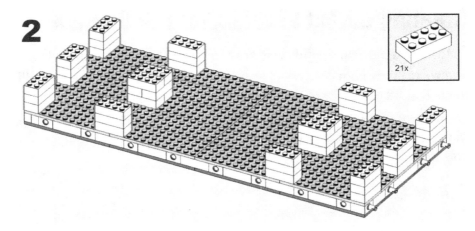

Figure 3-2. *Put the 2 × 4 bricks on the other side of the base*

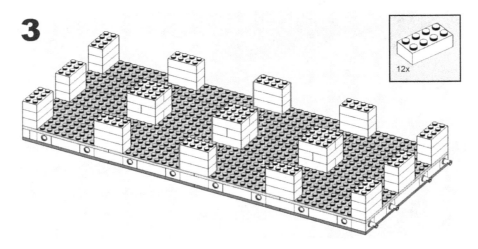

Figure 3-3. *Put the 2 × 4 bricks in the center of the base*

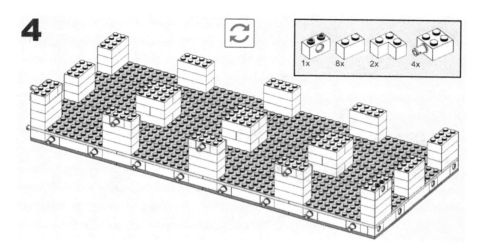

Figure 3-4. *Put on the 1 × 2 bricks, with the 2 × 2 corner bricks. Add on the 2 × 2 brick modified with connector pegs and the 1 × 2 technic brick with hole*

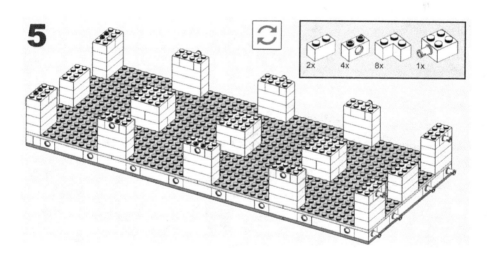

Figure 3-5. *Put on the 1 × 2 bricks, with the 2 × 2 corner bricks. Add on the 2 × 2 brick modified with connector peg and the 1 × 2 technic bricks with hole*

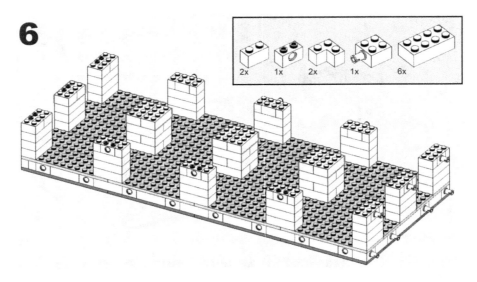

Figure 3-6. *Put on the 1 × 2 bricks, with the 2 × 2 corner bricks. Add on the 2 × 2 brick modified with connector peg and the 1 × 2 technic bricks with hole. Add on the 2 × 4 bricks in the middle*

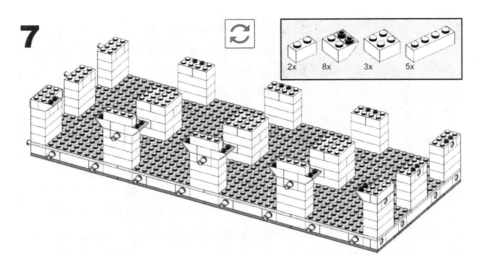

Figure 3-7. *Use the slope inverted 45 2 × 2, and then add on the 1 × 2, 2 × 2, and 1 × 4 bricks*

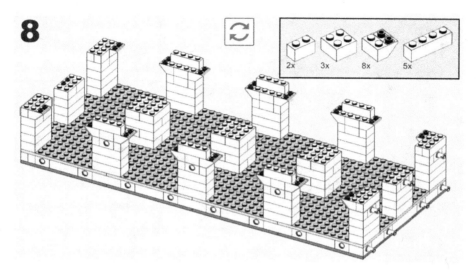

Figure 3-8. *Use the slope inverted 45 2 × 2, and then add on the 1 × 2, 2 × 2, and 1 × 4 bricks*

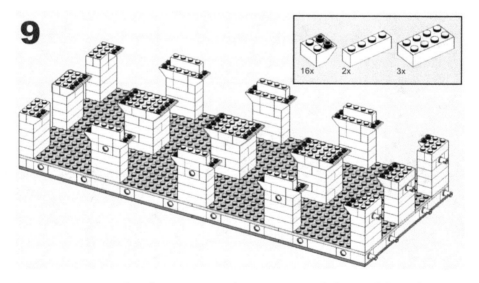

Figure 3-9. *Use the slope inverted 45 2 × 2, and then add on the 1 × 4 and 2 × 4 bricks*

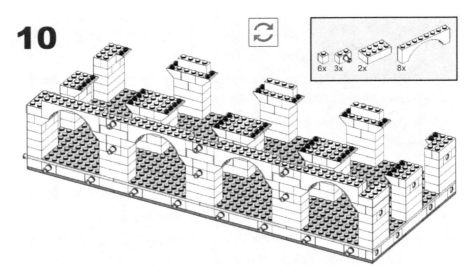

Figure 3-10. *Use the 1 × 1 and 2 × 4 bricks. Insert the modified 1 × 2 bricks with connector peg and the arch 1 × 8 × 2*

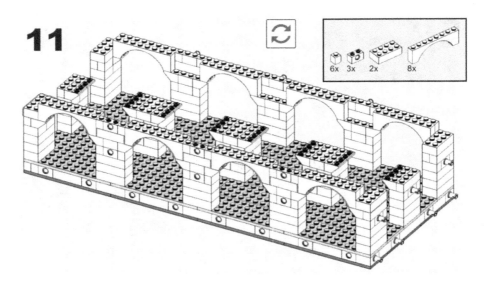

Figure 3-11. *Use the 1 × 1 and 2 × 4 bricks. Insert the modified 1 × 2 bricks with hole and the arch 1 × 8 × 2*

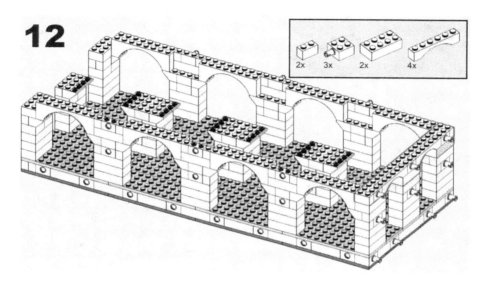

Figure 3-12. *Use the 1 × 2 and 2 × 4 bricks. Insert the modified 2 × 2 bricks with connector peg and the arch 1 × 6*

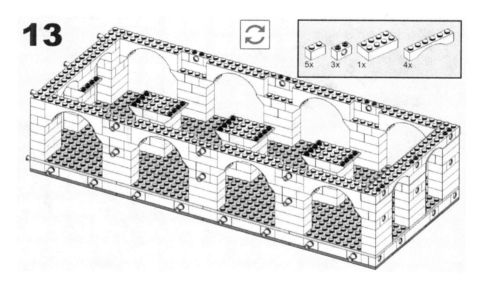

Figure 3-13. *Use the 1 × 2 and 2 × 4 bricks. Insert the modified 1 × 2 bricks with hole and the arch 1 × 6*

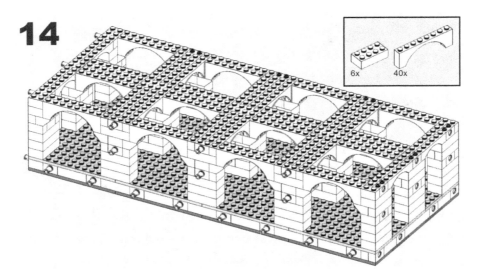

Figure 3-14. *Put on the arch 1 × 8 × 2 in the center, and then put on the 2 × 4 bricks*

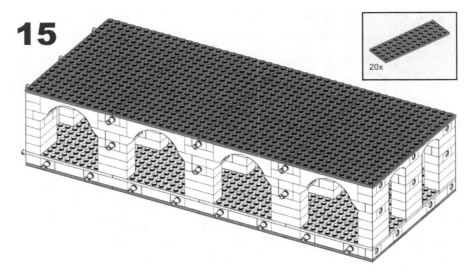

Figure 3-15. *Time to cap off the top with several 4 × 12 plates*

All right, you now have a second level, and you will notice that it has arches in it and there is some room to put things underneath the second level if you wish. However, you will need to connect that one with the other so the minifigures and their vehicles can go from one level to the other.

For the purposes of this instruction and simplicity, I'm going to recommend just building the base from Chapter 2 and attaching it at the bottom.

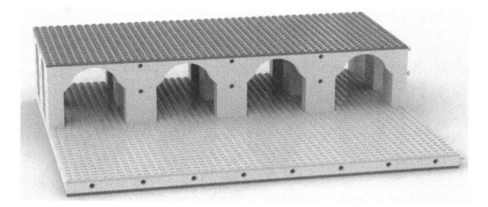

Figure 3-16. *The base from Chapter 2, with another level*

Building a Ramp

Okay, now that we have two levels, let us concentrate on putting ramps to the next one. This particular ramp is about 20 studs wide, which is enough to make a double-lane road for LEGO vehicles, which will be discussed in later chapters.

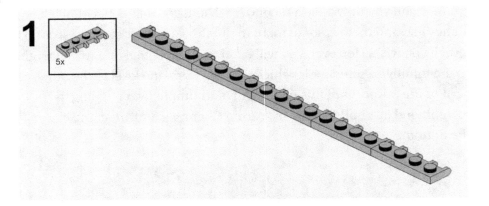

Figure 3-17. *Start by putting these 1 × 4 hinge plates together*

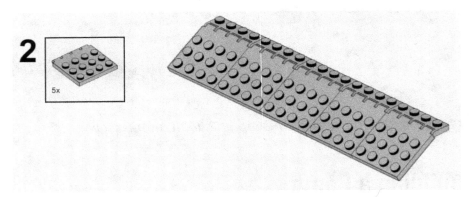

Figure 3-18. *Put on the 4 × 4 hinge vehicle roof pieces on this, and they should be angled at about 30 degrees*

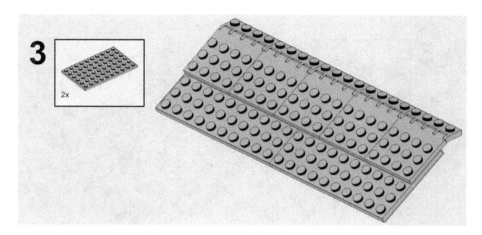

Figure 3-19. *Put on the 6 × 10 plates and put them underneath the hinges. It will join them together*

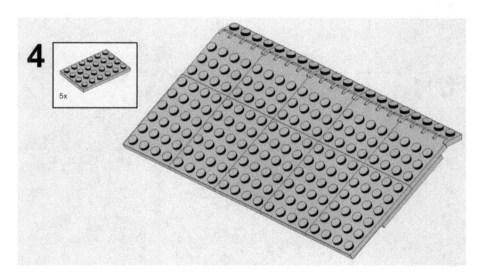

Figure 3-20. *The five 4 × 6 plates go on top, and they are at the same level of the 4 × 4 hinge pieces*

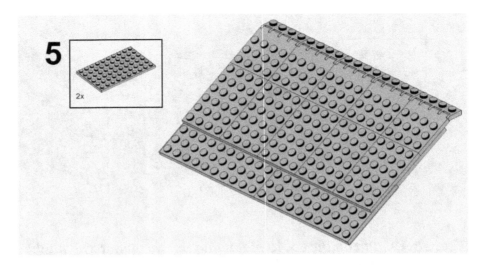

Figure 3-21. *Using two 6 × 10 plates, join the other 4 × 6 plates from the last step*

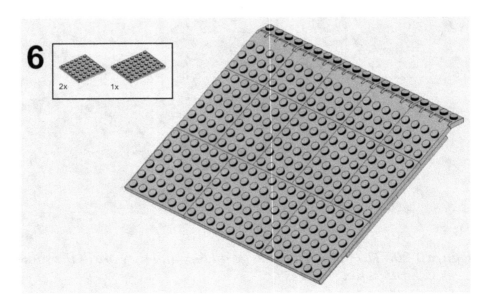

Figure 3-22. *Time to put on the two 6 × 6 plates and then the 6 × 8 plate in the middle*

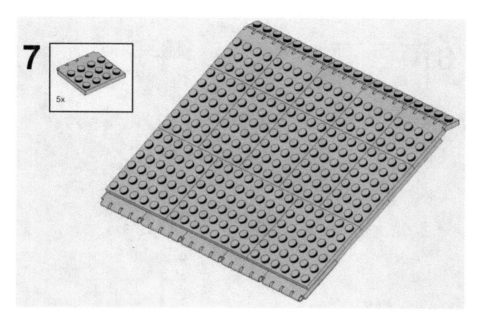

Figure 3-23. *Put on the 4 × 4 hinge vehicle roof pieces on the bottom this time*

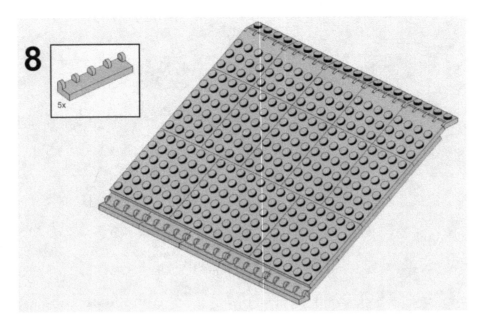

Figure 3-24. *Put on the 1 × 4 hinge pieces, and do a 30 degree bend in the other direction*

Once you have finished that ramp, make another one, and then put it on the base. But before you do that, know that this ramp will join the second ramp with its next level with a lower ramp. I recommend bringing some kind of support, even if it is not attached to the structure in any way. So let's make some of those.

Support for the Ramps

This is how to create some support for the ramp, which is needed for most LEGO projects.

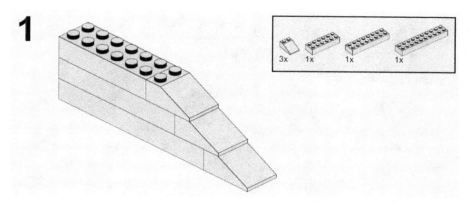

Figure 3-25. *Start with a slope 33 3 × 2 with a brick 2 × 10. Put another slope and 2 × 8 brick atop of that, and then follow that up with a slope and 2 × 6 atop of that*

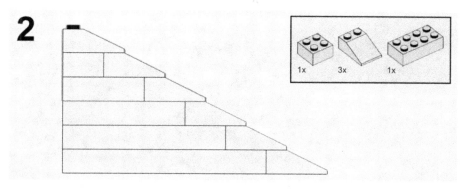

Figure 3-26. *Put a slope 33 3 × 2 and 2 × 4 brick on the creation. Then put another slope and 2 × 2 brick on that, and top it off with another slope*

Now, all you need to do is build three more of these, and you have support. Go ahead and put them down as follows.

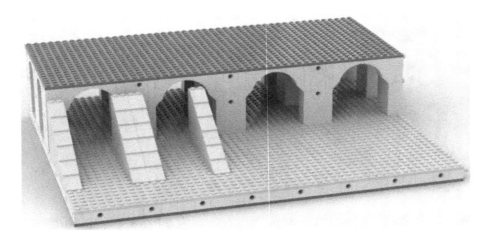

Figure 3-27. *A place to put the supports for the ramp*

Then, all you need to do is put the ramp on top of it.

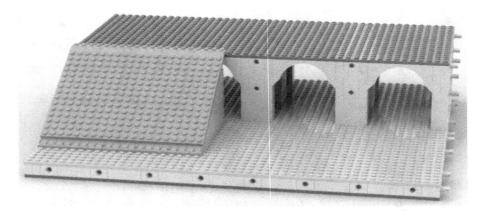

Figure 3-28. *With the ramp on, to create a way to join the top and bottom levels*

Creating New Terrain

Creating that LEGO ramp and its supports is not very difficult, but one of the hardest things to create is something that is, for lack of a better word, lifelike. When it comes to making rocks or a realistic hillside, you will run into some challenges. The first is the number of pieces, and LEGO created these rock pieces to fill in the gaps and create something that looks like rock.

Fortunately, LEGO makes pieces that are essentially hollowed out pieces of rock, and they could be used on their own, I recommend using them as a place to start, and then build up on them until it looks like realistic terrain.

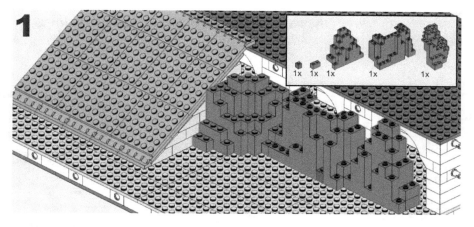

Figure 3-29. *Go ahead and put the 8 × 8 × 6, 4 × 10 × 6, and 3 × 8 × 7 rock panels on with the 1 × 1 and 1 × 2 bricks*

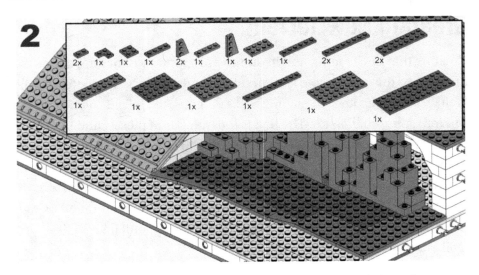

Figure 3-30. *Put in the various blue LEGO plates and then the green LEGO plates with the wedges*

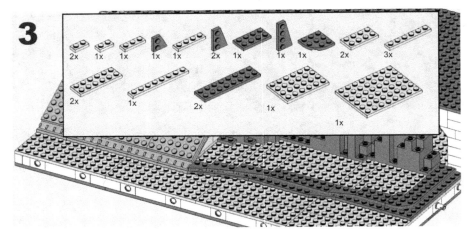

Figure 3-31. *Put in the yellow LEGO plates, and then put on the green plates, wedge plates, and the round plate*

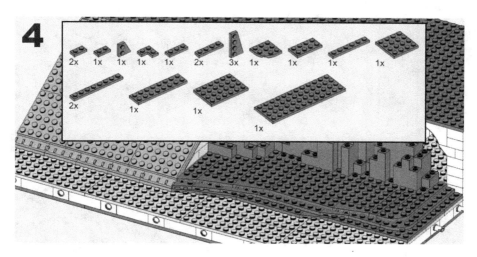

Figure 3-32. *Put on the red LEGO plates, and then put on the green LEGO plates, wedge plates, and the round corner plates*

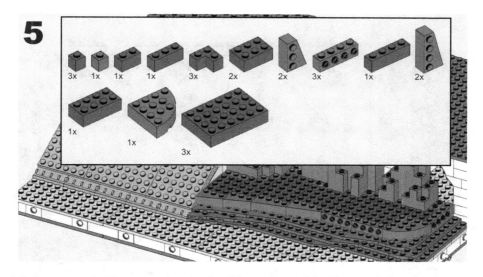

Figure 3-33. *Time to put on the blue LEGO blocks, and then put on the green wedges, three modified 1 × 4 with studs on the side bricks, the 1 × 1 brick, and the 4 × 4 round corner brick*

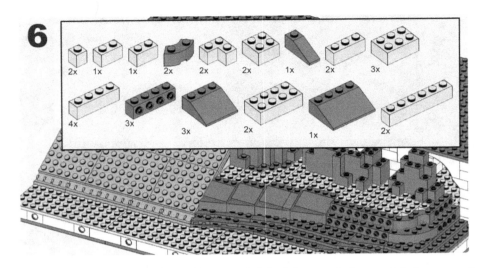

Figure 3-34. *Put on the yellow LEGO bricks, and then add the round corner 2 × 2 bricks, the modified 1 × 4 bricks with studs on the side, and the various slopes*

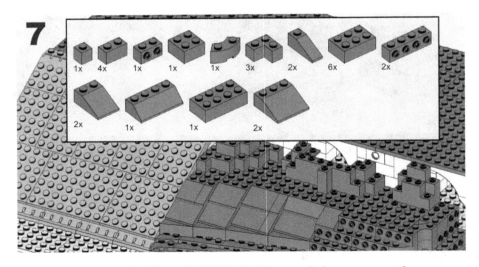

Figure 3-35. *Put in the red LEGO bricks, and then put on the green round 2 × 2 brick, the slopes, the 2 × 2 brick, and the modified bricks with studs on the side*

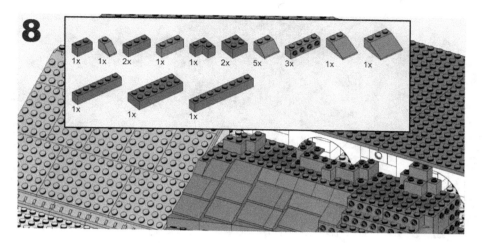

Figure 3-36. *Put on the blue LEGO bricks, and then put on the green slopes, the 1 × 3 brick, and the three 1 × 4 modified bricks with studs on the side*

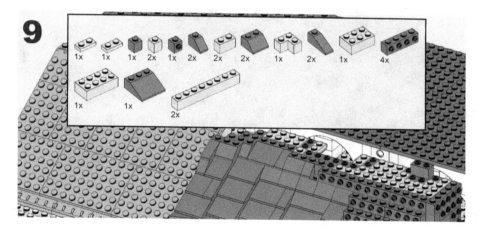

Figure 3-37. *Put on the yellow LEGO bricks, and then put on the green 1 × 1 brick, the modified bricks with studs on the side, and the slopes*

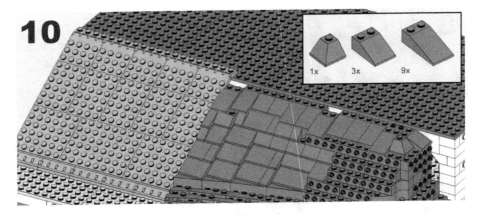

Figure 3-38.   *Time to put on the 18 4 × 2 slopes, the 33 3 × 2 slopes, and the 45 slope 2 × 2 double convex corner*

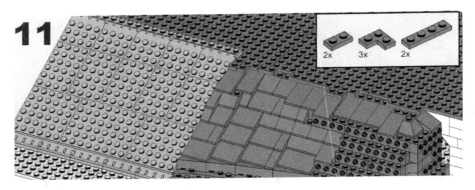

Figure 3-39.   *Put on the 1 × 2, 1 × 4, and 2 × 2 corner plates*

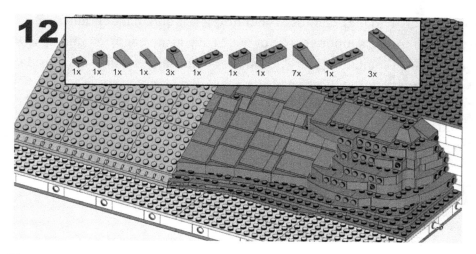

Figure 3-40. *Put on all the LEGO bricks, the slopes, curved slopes, and the plates*

Now, I used green LEGO pieces to create what I believe to be a realistic hillside, but if you want, you can use gray, brown, or other colors to convey what it is you are going for like a more rocky terrain. It really is all about just trying things out and seeing what seems like something nature would create and then going from there.

Conclusion

On building a LEGO base, it might be necessary to take it to the next level if you want to create a land with hills and other levels. It is highly recommended to build your next levels with lots of support, so more models can be put on them without fear of anything crumbling.

It is great to make ramps to your next levels and make certain that these ramps are supported. Not only that, if you are going to build up a next level of something like a hillside, try to make it as much as a hillside as possible with the application of some textured blocky styles.

These last two chapters have given you the skills for a foundation of land to build your LEGO creations on, but the next few chapters are going to be devoted to things that are man-made, such as houses and vehicles.

CHAPTER 4

Creating a LEGO House and Any Other Multistory Building

If you think back to your very first memories of LEGO building, chances are, your first big project was most likely a house. I remember building with one of the earliest basic sets and working with my father to construct a house that we saw on the back of the box. At that time, it seemed very difficult, but in comparison to building a real house, it is very simple.

There was a time when I was young when we moved into a house made from scratch, and for many months, nothing really seemed to happen. I remember looking at the plot of land and thinking: "there's no way you could put a house here over the summertime." In many ways, I was correct, because there were delays and the house didn't really get to its liveable stage until late September/early October.

During that time, I got to see giant holes being dug, and then wood placed around it with lots of rebar in the middle. Then, it was just a concrete slab that was a basement, with lots of pipe and electrical conduit being laid around it.

Then came one day when people in semitrucks and flatbed vehicles arrived, and they actually had the house in very giant pieces. I remember watching them in the space of a day put all the giant pieces in place that

© Mark Rollins 2024
M. Rollins, *Ultimate LEGO Worldbuilding and Architecture*, Maker Innovations Series,
https://doi.org/10.1007/979-8-8688-0521-9_4

would eventually be the house. It is really quite something, and I hope that as you build your own LEGO constructions, you will feel the same sense of completion.

Not only will this chapter show you how to create a house, but give you the knowhow to build an entire town of buildings of all kinds of various purposes.

Constructing a Basic LEGO House

After all, if you want to build a real house, then you have to make certain the land is even buildable in the first place, then you have to dig up a lot of earth in order to pour a lot of concrete foundations. Even when building the walls, you also have to plan its infrastructure from the plumbing to electricity, not to mention the heating, cooling, and other ventilation systems.

I have to admit that a LEGO house is much simpler as you don't need to worry about all of the infrastructure details of a real house. All you need is a solid foundation, which is why I have spent the last two chapters focusing on that. As I have said before, you are free to start with a basic baseplate and work from there.

Still, the foundation is key as it will give you the basic area where you can determine the dimensions of your house. I split up the giant foundation into several distinct areas, as I felt that these could serve as property boundaries. In combining ten 4 × 12 plates in a two-by-five formation, this gives you somewhat adequate room to start constructing a house.

Given elementary rules for finding the area in a given space, length times width, then we can use the studs to figure out how much room is going to be in the house itself once the walls are formed.

I decided to remove two studs off the top of it in order to create a "front yard." Granted, there isn't much one can do in that allotment of space, but if nothing else, it will give a bit of a buffer zone between the road and the house. If you think about it, there should be quite a bit of room between them, and all two studs of room really does is create a very skinny sidewalk. Of course, you can design your creation to have a big front yard and backyard, but I'm going to be focusing more on the actual building rather than the land.

So, with two studs shaven off, the actual area of the house itself is also going to be shortened by the presence of the walls. Granted, it is possible to use panel-type pieces to give a little more space, but you might not be able to change these big pieces when you want to. It is possible to put utilitarian functions on the walls as you build, but I will focus more on that in Chapter 10. Still, your LEGO minifigs won't be able to pass through the walls unless they are ghosts, so be certain to have doors or at least openings between rooms.

What you are looking at is something that is 16 × 18, which is 288 square feet worth of studs in four walls. Yes, that doesn't sound like a lot, and if we use the rule of one stud = one foot, then you should know that according to US Census data, the average newly built single-family home in 2022 was approximately 2,300 square feet.

Yes, this type of home will be packed, and I have lived in both large and small homes. For almost two decades, I lived in a trailer and my wife and I had three kids in this small space. I actually don't want to calculate the square footage of that, because I'm surprised we ever could have lived there.

Also, if you are going to look at a house, it is going to have distinct rooms. Yes, I am going to spend some time focusing on how to make a house that is more than just a façade. I understand that the goal of this book is to create a LEGO world that can be put on display, and I also understand that most people don't look too closely at what is inside the LEGO creation. However, this book is about how to create a world that minifigures can be comfortable in, so yes, I actually account for the number of bathrooms. Yes, I will actually show how to create a LEGO toilet, but you'll have to wait until the next chapter.

Now, when it comes to deciding how to make rooms in your LEGO house, I highly recommend the art of napkin sketches. If you aren't familiar with napkin sketches, then just know that they are simple drawings of a single idea, without going into too much detail without how it all works. I'm going to assume that this practice started with architects discussing ideas over lunch, and paper napkins are the easiest thing to sketch on before the proliferation of smartphones and smart tablets.

I bring this up because you can use a napkin sketch to form a rudimentary plan as far as how your rooms will be organized. I figure if you are going to build a house that is made for one, then you will probably want to have a room for a bedroom and a bathroom as well. I will be discussing furniture in later chapters, but for now, let's just get a good sketch going on.

There's going to be a few things that I am going to want in a house designed for living one's daily life, such as a bedroom, bathroom, living room, and kitchen. To conserve space, I opted for the living room and kitchen to be essentially one room, without any walls in between. I'm not quite thinking of furniture at this particular point.

I do have to be thinking of the placement of doors, and I definitely want one on the bedroom and bathroom. I might actually want a doorway between the bathroom and bedroom, but I found that this was impossible once I started putting in furniture. When it comes to building any type of building, there are a lot of good pieces to have.

Doors

You're always going to need a door if you are going to build any building, because how else are those minifigs going to go through.

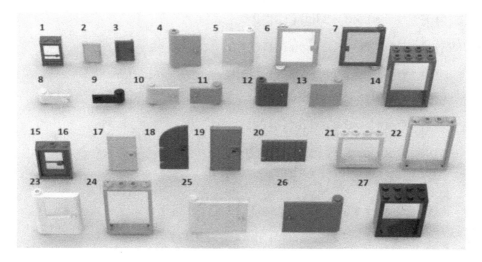

Figure 4-1. *Samples of LEGO door pieces*

1) Door 1 × 2 × 3 hinge on left with solid studs and fixed glass (32ac01)

2) Door 1 × 2 × 3 with vertical handle, mold for tabless frames (60614)

3) Door 1 × 2 × 3 with vertical handle (6546)

4) Door 1 × 3 × 4 left open between top and bottom hinge (58381)

5) Door 1 × 3 × 4 right open between top and bottom hinge (58380)

6) Door 1 × 3 × 5 left with trans-clear glass (73436c01)

7) Door 1 × 3 × 5 right with trans-brown glass (73435c03)

8) Door 1 × 3 × 1 left (3822)

9) Door 1 × 3 × 1 right (3821)

10)   Door 1 × 3 × 2 left (3189)

11)   Door 1 × 3 × 2 right (3188)

12)   Door 1 × 3 × 3 left open Between top and bottom hinge (60658)

13)   Door 1 × 3 × 3 right (3192)

14)   Door frame 2 × 4 × 6 (60599)

15)   Door frame 1 × 3 × 4 (3579)

16)   Door 1 × 3 × 4 with glass (7930)

17)   Door 1 × 3 × 5 with stud handle (2657)

18)   Door 1 × 3 × 6 curved top (2554)

19)   Door 1 × 3 × 6 with stud handle (80683)

20)   Door 1 × 4 × 3 (6078)

21)   Door frame 1 × 4 × 4 lift

22)   Door frame 1 × 4 × 6 with 2 holes on top and bottom (60596)

23)   Door 1 × 4 × 5 train left, thin support on bottom (4181)

24)   Door 1 × 4 × 6 with 2 holes on top and bottom (60596)

25)   Door 1 × 5 × 4 left (3195)

26)   Door 1 × 5 × 4 right (3194)

27)   Door frame 2 × 4 × 5 (4130)

Windows

If we are going to do doors, then we need to do windows as well.

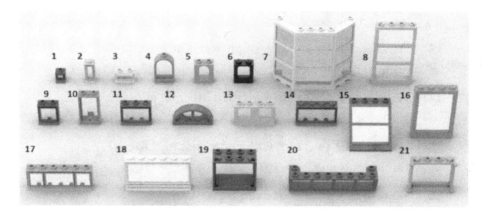

Figure 4-2. *Samples of LEGO window pieces*

1) Window 1 × 1 × 1 with extended lip (39b)

2) Window 1 × 1 × 2 with extended lip (29a)

3) Window 1 × 2 × 1 (27)

4) Window 1 × 2 × 2 2/3 with rounded top (30044)

5) Window 1 × 2 × 2 castle (90195)

6) Window 1 × 2 × 2 plane (2377)

7) Window 3 × 8 × 6 bay with trans-brown glass (30185c01)

8) Window 1 × 4 × 6 with 3 panes (57894)

9) Window 1 × 2 × 2 with extended lip and hole in top (7026b)

10) Window 1 × 2 × 3 flat front in stud (60593)

11) Window 1 × 3 × 2 with extended lip and hollow studs (31b)

12) Window 1 × 4 × 1 2/3 with spoked rounded top (20309)

13) Window 1 × 4 × 2 plane, single top hole and single bottom hole for glass (61345)

14) Window 1 × 4 × 2 with extended lip and solid studs (453a)

15) Window 4 × 4 × 3 roof with center bar and fixed trans-light blue glass (6159c01)

16) Window 1 × 4 × 5 with fixed glass (4347)

17) Window 1 × 6 × 2 (645)

18) Window 1 × 6 × 3 panorama with solid studs and fixed glass (604ac01)

19) Window 2 × 4 × 3 hollow studs (60598)

20) Window 2 × 8 × 2 boat (89648)

21) Window 1 × 4 × 3 (3853)

While I'm on the subject of doors as well as windows, this would be a good time to figure out where you want the front door. You can also plan out what type of windows that you want, and there is a good assortment to choose from.

The napkin sketch is the one that I am going to be following for the sake of this chapter, but of course, you can build your house as large as you want given the amount of pieces that you have. In fact, I highly recommend creating a napkin sketch that is too big for most napkins, and constructing it in Stud.io to see if it accounts for your all your needs. Granted, you don't necessarily need a napkin, and I just used a 3 × 5 card.

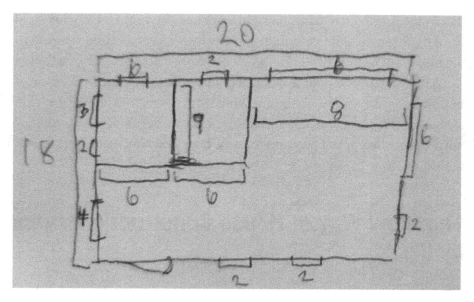

Figure 4-3. *A quick napkin sketch of a LEGO house*

This would be a good time to talk about structure in building a house. In Chapters 2 and 3, I talked about building methods that are necessary for a strong foundation, but I would recommend that many of these principles apply for building a house.

You will notice in the instructions below that the four walls of the house are designed to lock together on the edges. Also, levels are constructed with as much bricks interlocking as possible. When it comes to pieces like doors and possible windows, these will need to be locked in place with the roof, which will be quite a section in this chapter.

If you really want your house to be strong, you could build it with walls that are two studs thick. There are two advantages to this. First, if you are the type that is concerned about color, your interior of your home can have a different color than the outside of your house. After all, LEGO does not make bricks that have one color on one side, and a different color on the other. Unless you want to do some kind of paint job on the inside, which I do not recommend, two layers could work best for you. That means some thick doorframes, not to mention some windows with double layers, but the house will stand very strong when reinforced at the top.

A building that is built two layers thick will be advantageous when building a multiple-story building, which we will get into later. For now, let's discuss the basics of a LEGO house. There are several ways to make a house, and one is a fast way and the other is a slow way. Let's just start with the slow way.

The Slow Way of House Construction: Brick by Brick

I mentioned before in Chapter 1 how there was a move in LEGO sometime in the mid-1990s that shifted away from building homes on an individual brick-by-brick basis. I was a little off on that, because if you look at the discontinued sets of Fabuland, they were all about pre-fab structures that you can click together in a matter of minutes, and your home is done.

However, the earliest LEGO Castle sets were all brick-by-brick complex constructions, but later iterations just had very large panels. I have to admit, it is very easy to work with certain LEGO Castle sets that have pre-fab pieces. The issue with those large pieces is that is all they can be used for, but I want to talk about building a house from brick to slope or foundation to roof.

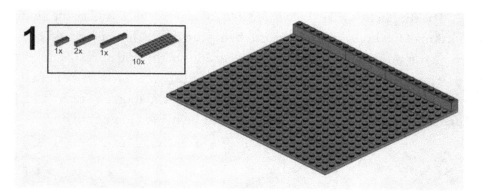

Figure 4-4. *The first step of building, with the bricks forming the back wall*

For this step, you do not need the ten 4 × 12 plates as a base for the house. I just put it here as kind of a reference, because you have to have something for a foundation here for the back portion of the wall of the house, something that will fit very well into the large two-story foundational base in Chapters 2 and 3. You could use a baseplate if you want, but the more stable, the better.

Speaking of stability, you will note that I apply the two-stud overlap rule in building the back wall, something that I will try and adhere to as often as I can to make certain things are structurally sound.

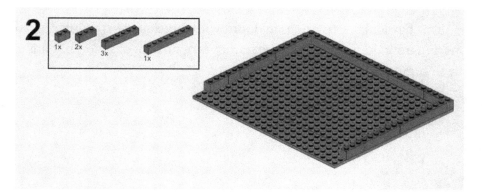

Figure 4-5. *Forming the side walls of the house*

For simplicity's sake, I have decided to refer the back wall as the south portion of the house, with the north being the front. This step would be about the side walls, or west and east portions of the house, respectfully.

There are reasons why they are not identical, which will be clear in the next few steps. Using the ten 4 × 12 plates as a foundation will result in a one-stud overlap at best, which can't really be helped in many cases.

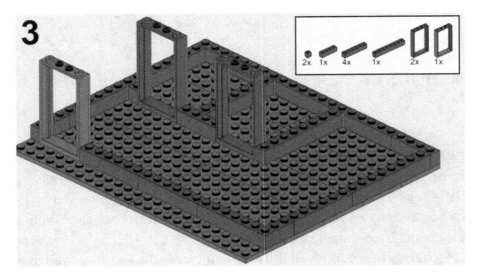

Figure 4-6. *The north part of the house has begun, as well as the walls of the interior rooms*

This particular step brings in doors, with three used in the interior, and one as a front doors. Note that the frames take up a lot of space, but this is the minimum required for a minifig entry.

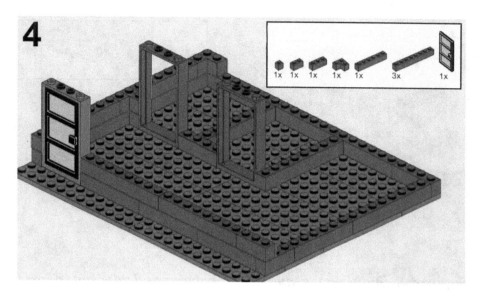

Figure 4-7. *Building up the west side as well as the south*

The best part about building a LEGO house is how much you are not limited to as far as design is concerned. This is the style of door I chose for the front, but you can make another type if you choose. You are also not limited to one color of the house if you like, creating a stripped effect of using one color for one level and then switch to a different color for the next level. I simply chose blue because that was the color that I had the most of when I first started playing with LEGO as a kid.

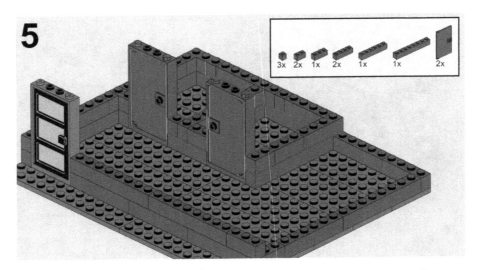

Figure 4-8. *Build up the interior of the rooms and add some doors*

You will notice that as the walls start to build up levels, I will often use corner bricks or some kind of overlap just so no wall isn't linked to the house in some way. I highly recommend doing that unless you want the wall to be easily removable.

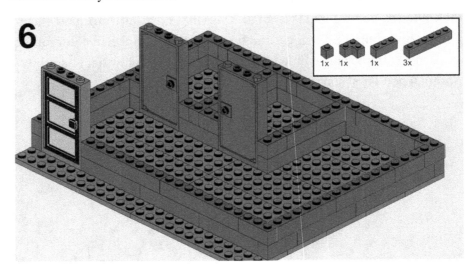

Figure 4-9. *Finish the next layer of the north wall and the next of the east wall*

The two doors are the entrances to the bedroom and bathroom. Now that the first two layers are done, it is time to get decorative and start adding windows.

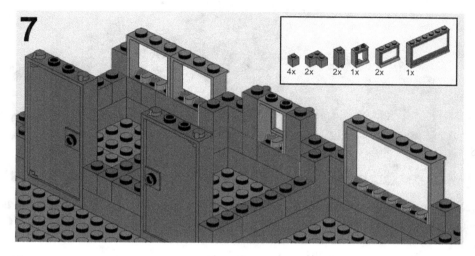

Figure 4-10. *The south side of the house is built up with both walls and windows*

You will note that some of my windows have these 1 × 2 × 2 pieces, and these are used to hold shutters that will be added on later. You are more than welcome to use more windows than this, especially if you want viewers to peer inside a detailed home. Keep in mind that there could be structural issues.

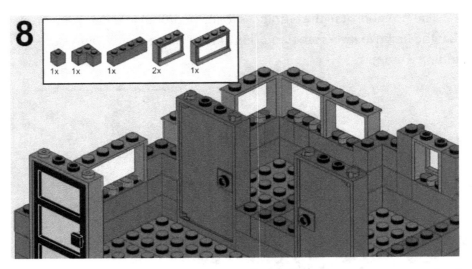

Figure 4-11. *Time to start building up the west side of the house with windows and bricks*

Again, there are really a lot of windows that can be used, and this is where you can get very creative.

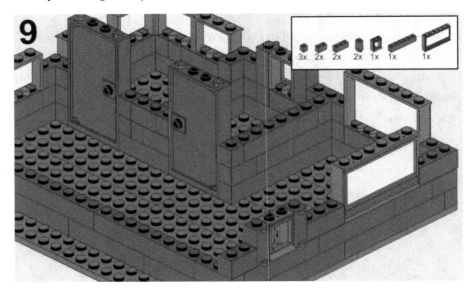

Figure 4-12. *Build up the interiors as well as the east side of the house, with windows and shutters*

The one thing that I can't really teach in this book is how to give a house a sense of character. I leave that entirely up to you, but I think that I put quite a few windows on this one, maybe more than average.

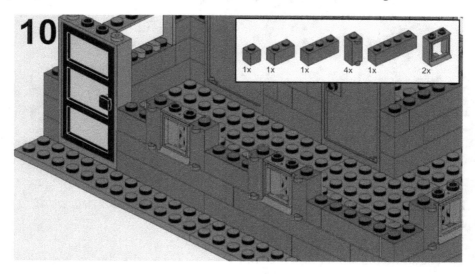

Figure 4-13. *Build another level on the north side of the house, with windows and shutter holders*

I put a minimum amount of windows here and gave them shutters because I guess I like my privacy.

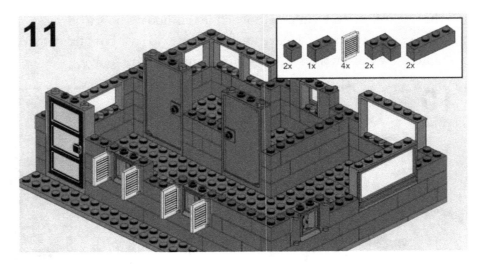

Figure 4-14. *Time to build up in between the windows and adding the shutters*

For some reason, I think the shutters only work with the 2 × 2 window pieces, but I could be wrong. Maybe LEGO needs to create curtains.

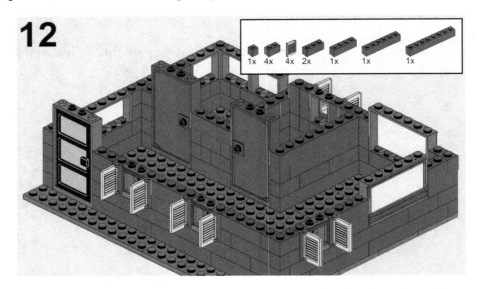

Figure 4-15. *With the application of some bricks, the fourth wall level is complete*

This might be a good time to say that I really went plain with this house, with only one color and the smooth type of brick. There are bricks that have a brick pattern on them and could be used, but I wasn't certain if it fit with the house aesthetically.

You will also notice that this is your basic house, with everything being at right angles. Many fancier houses have a lot of curvaceous structures to them, not to mention very liberal uses of glass. Still, most homes tend to be like boxes, and I suppose that I might be wrong by putting the emphasis of that here. I recommend looking at some of LEGO's townhouses for their unusual styles of architecture, as well as their painstaking attention to detail.

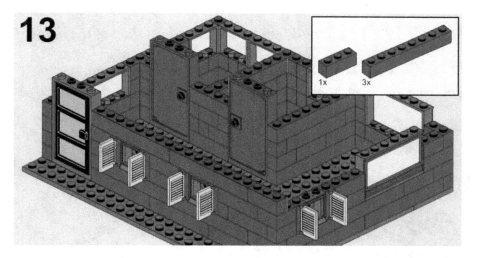

Figure 4-16. *Time to start building up the fifth level on the north side and add a level to the interior*

This is probably a good time for me to discuss how difficult it can be to get the illustrations to show a LEGO house at certain angles. I did my best on that, and I hope that you can easily see what has to be done next.

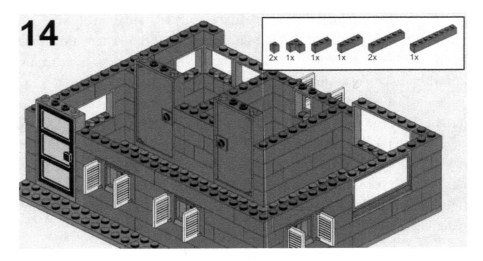

Figure 4-17. *Time to build up the west and east sides of the house*

At this point, we are at the tops of the higher windows and starting to get to the roof level. There are still a few more steps to go, though.

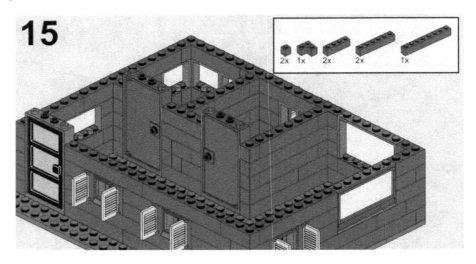

Figure 4-18. *It is time to build up the levels in between and around the rooms*

I should also point out that a lot of home have things built into the walls such as spaceheaters and other such utilitarian things, but this home is bare minimum. You might want to plan out your home in advance if you wish to add such things.

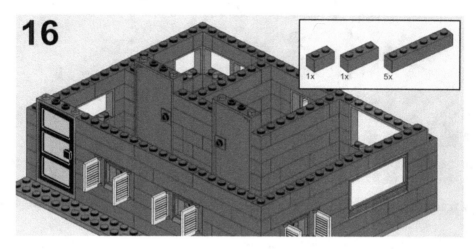

Figure 4-19. *Time for the sixth brick level on the north and east walls*

At this, it gets to the top, and some more decorative trim can be added if you wish.

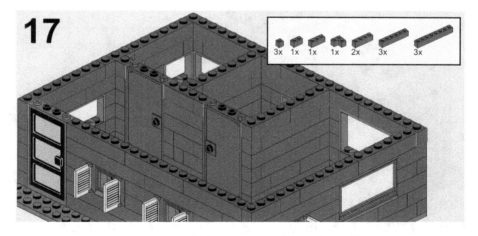

Figure 4-20. *Time to cap off the west and north walls*

At this time, the bricks are at the top of the door, but it is still not done.

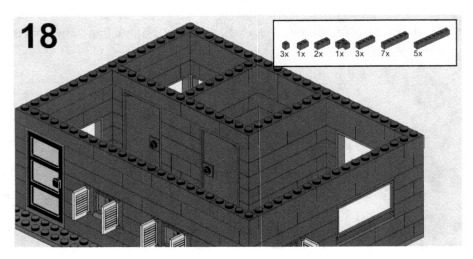

Figure 4-21. *This is where you just build up another level in the house*

Even though a minifig can easily stand in a section six or even five bricks high, it is good to add yet another layer.

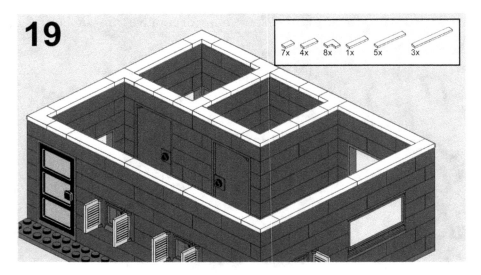

Figure 4-22. *This is where you add a layer of tiles to the top to secure it in place. The corner tile pieces really help to keep it together*

The Roof of the LEGO House

So now that the house is done, it is time to put on the roof, and it is recommended that you make a roof that is easily removable, which is why walls of the house in the previous section use a lot of tile.

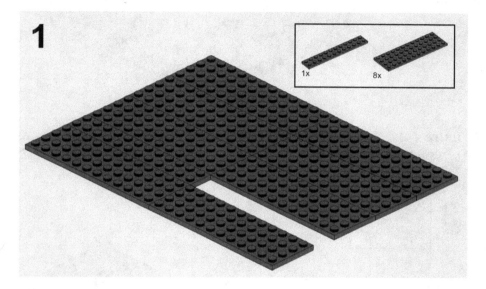

Figure 4-23. *Laying down the base of the roof with these 4 × 12 plates and one 2 × 12 plate, the gap left in deliberately*

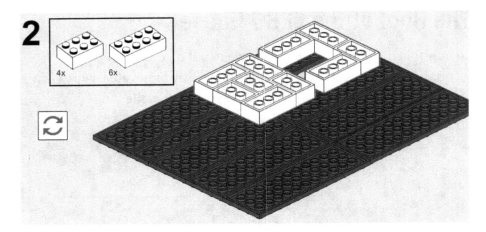

Figure 4-24. *Use the 2 × 3 and 2 × 4 bricks to hold some of the plates from step 1 together*

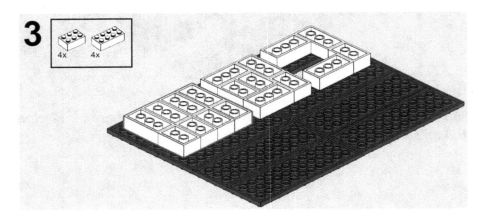

Figure 4-25. *Use the 2 × 3 and 2 × 4 bricks for some greater stability*

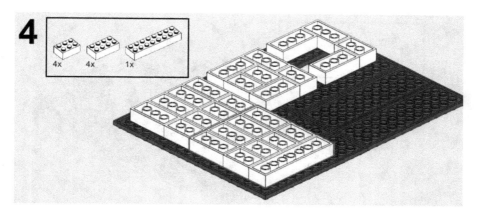

Figure 4-26. *This is the step where one side of the underbelly of the roof gets completed with the help of the 2 × 3, 2 × 4, and 2 × 8 bricks*

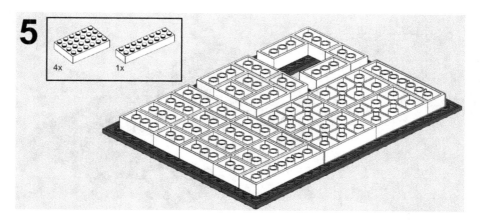

Figure 4-27. *More of the 4 × 6 bricks with a 2 × 8 brick really hold it together*

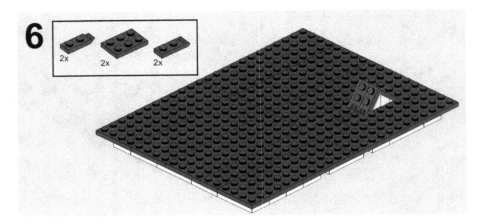

Figure 4-28. *Put on the 2 × 3 plates with these hinges that form an entrance to an attic*

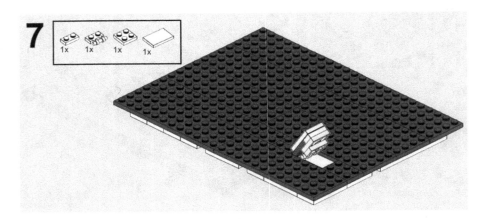

Figure 4-29. *Put on tiles and plates to form this entrance of an attic opening*

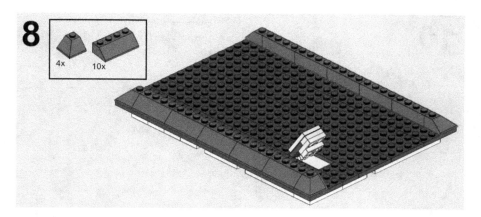

Figure 4-30. *Time to start the roof with some slope pieces*

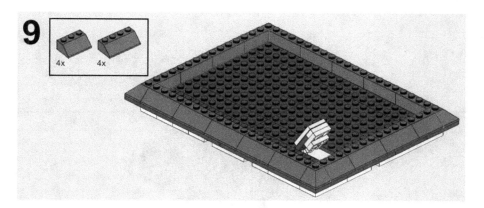

Figure 4-31. *Time to put on the slopes on the sides to finish the sloped portion of the roof*

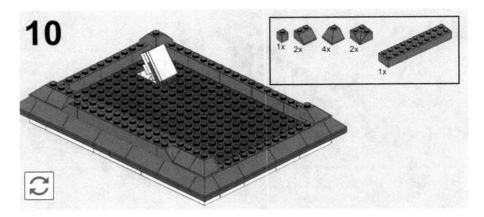

Figure 4-32. *Put on the another level with some slope pieces that start the roof slanting in an interesting direction*

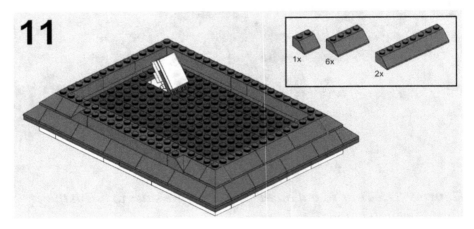

Figure 4-33. *Time to complete another level of the sloped part of the roof*

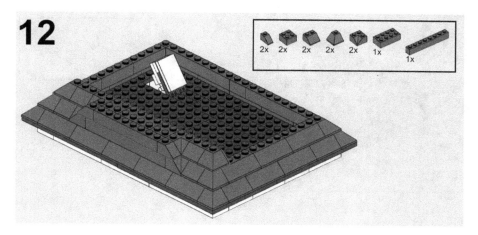

Figure 4-34. *Add another side to this section of the roof*

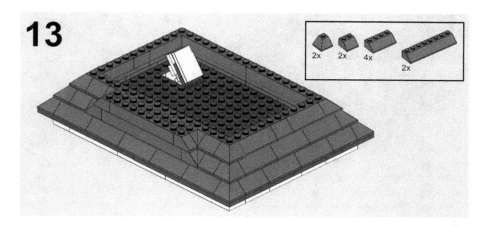

Figure 4-35. *Finish building up another portion of the roof*

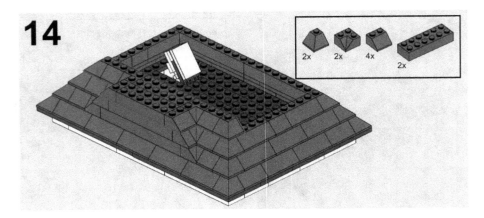

Figure 4-36. *Add another level to the framing of the house*

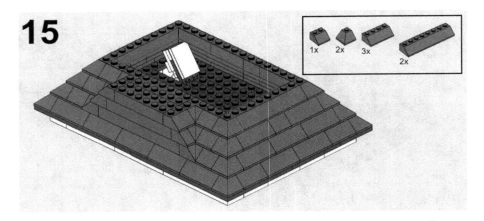

Figure 4-37. *Complete another layer on the roof*

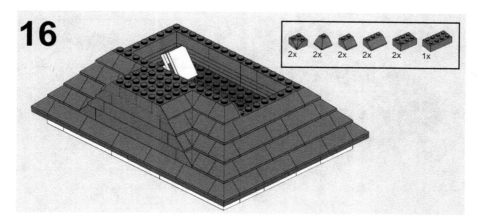

Figure 4-38. *Add on another section to the side of the roof as shown*

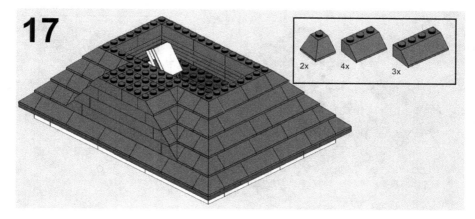

Figure 4-39. *Put on more sloped bricks as it comes closer to the top*

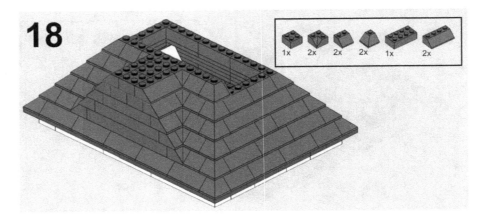

Figure 4-40. *The top of the roof is now nearing completion*

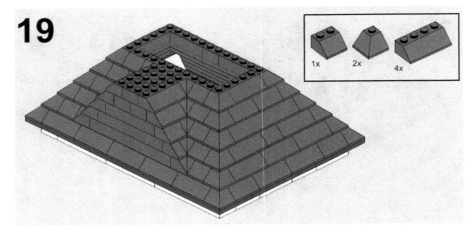

Figure 4-41. *Time to add on another side as the roof becomes more complete*

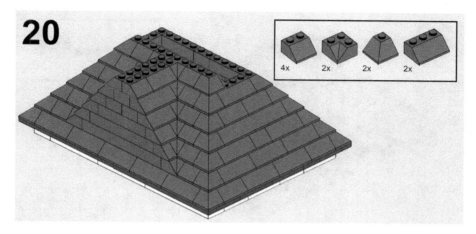

Figure 4-42. *Keep building up the side of the house*

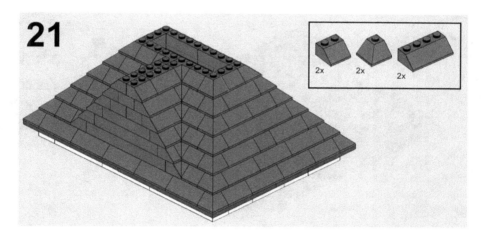

Figure 4-43. *It is another time to build up the side of the house*

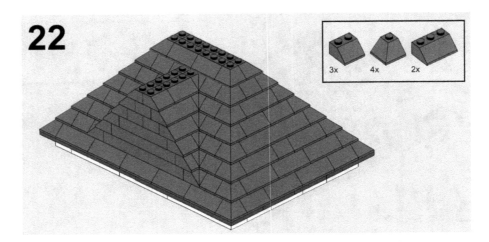

Figure 4-44. *Cap off the roof with the slopes from this step*

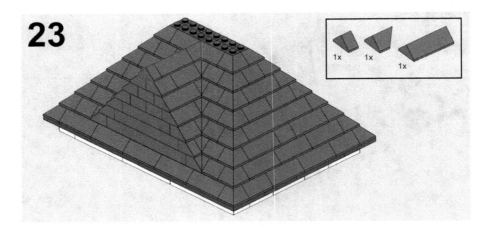

Figure 4-45. *The side section can be capped off with these pieces*

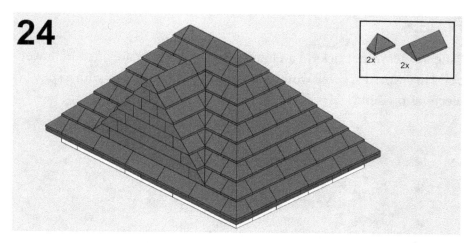

Figure 4-46. *Another section of the roof gets capped off as follows*

Okay, now that the roof is done, just put it on the house and it is complete. See Chapter 10 if you want to check that out, but for now, let's shift gears, like a faster gear for building.

The Fast Way of LEGO House Building: Panels and Other Pieces

So, I spent a lot of time talking about the slow way to create a house, with bricks and layers with a roof to cap it all off. Now, I am going to talk about how easy it is to use pre-fab pieces to create a very quick building or domicile and talk about how this can be multiple stories.

Remember at the beginning of this chapter where I talked about how a real house that I lived in was made of pre-fab pieces that were put together in the space of about a day? Well, they didn't just drop them into place like LEGO pieces, but they were secured into place. I definitely recommend you secure yours into place, and I do give examples as the structure is built. I recommend the panels and cylinders, and here are some good examples of them in action.

143

Panels

Panels differ from bricks in an interesting way as they are often hollowed out. They work very well when you need to build up a wall with as few pieces as possible.

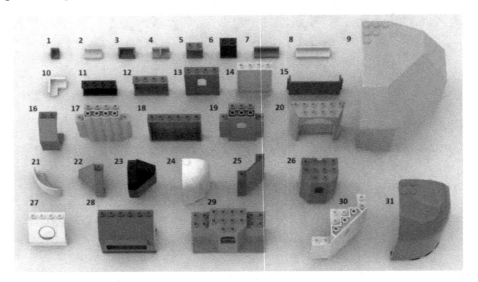

Figure 4-47. *Samples of LEGO panels*

1) Panel 1 × 1 × 1 corner (6231)

2) Panel 1 × 2 × 1 (4865)

3) Panel 1 × 2 × 1 with rounded corners and 2 sides (23969)

4) Panel 1 × 2 × 1 with rounded corners and center divider (93095)

5) Panel 1 × 2 × 2 hollow studs (4864b)

6) Panel 1 × 2 × 3 hollow studs (2362b)

7) Panel 1 × 3 × 1 (23950)

8)   Panel 1 × 4 × 1 (30413)

9)   Panel 10 × 10 × 12 quarter dome (2409)

10)   Panel 2 × 2 × 1 corner (91501)

11)   Panel 1 × 4 × 2 with side supports hollow studs (14718)

12)   Panel 1 × 4 × 3 with side supports hollow studs (60581)

13)   Panel 1 × 4 × 5 wall with window (60808)

14)   Panel 1 × 4 × 6 wavy (34732)

15)   Panel 1 × 6 × 3 with studs on the sides (98280)

16)   Panel 3 × 2 × 6 (2466)

17)   Panel 2 × 6 × 6 with log profile (30140)

18)   Panel 1 × 6 × 5 (59349)

19)   Panel 2 × 5 × 6 wall with window (4444)

20)   Panel 2 × 6 × 6 wall with gothic arch (35565)

21)   Panel 3 × 2 × 2 corner convex (3535)

22)   Panel 3 × 3 × 3 corner convex (30079)

23)   Panel 3 × 3 × 6 corner convex (2468)

24)   Panel 2 × 3 × 6 corner convex with curved top (6059)

25)   Panel 3 × 3 × 6 corner wall without bottom indentations (87241)

26)   Panel 3 × 4 × 6 turret wall with window (30246)

27)   Panel 4 × 3 × 3 trans-light blue porthole (30080c01)

28)   Panel 3 x 6 x 6 Sloped with Window (30288)

29)   Panel 3 × 8 × 6 with window (48490)

30)   Panel 6 × 6 × 6 corner with window (6055)

31)   Panel 6 × 6 × 9 corner convex with curved top (6002)

Cylinders

These are different from the round bricks and tiles, as it covers a lot of volume. They are useful if you want to create some more circular or curvaceous looks to your house.

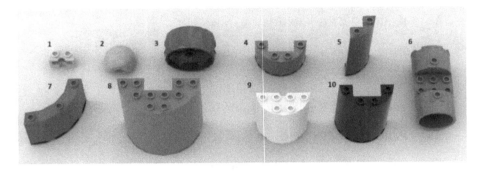

Figure 4-48. *Samples of LEGO cylinders*

1)   Cylinder half 1 × 2 × 1 (68013)

2)   Cylinder hemisphere 2 × 2 with cutout (61287)

3)   Cylinder hemisphere 4 × 4 × 1 2/3 with peg holes and center bar (41531)

4)   Cylinder half 2 × 4 × 2 with 1 × 2 cutout (24593)

5)   Cylinder quarter 2 × 2 × 5 with 1 × 1 cutout (30987)

6)   Cylinder 3 × 6 × 2 2/3 horizontal round connections between interior studs (30360)

7)   Cylinder quarter 4 × 4 × 3 (4041)

8)   Cylinder half 3 × 6 × 6 with 1 × 2 cutout (87926)

9) Cylinder half 2 × 4 × 4 (6259)

10) Cylinder half 2 × 4 × 5 with 1 × 2 cutout (85941)

Support and Roofs

So, this is some interesting pieces that could be used if you are creating a larger house than the ones that I use as samples here in this chapter, but I leave that entirely up to you.

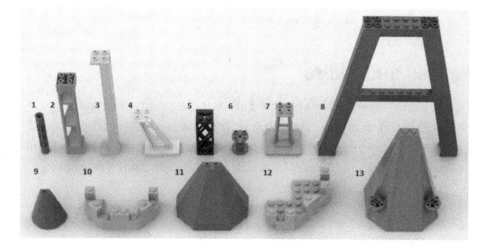

Figure 4-49. *Samples of support and roofs in LEGO*

1) Support 1 × 1 × 5 1/3 spiral staircase axle (40244)

2) Support 2 × 2 × 10 girder triangular vertical (30517)

3) Support 2 × 2 × 13 with 5 pin holes (91176)

4) Support 2 × 4 × 5 stanchion inclined 5 mm wide posts (4476b)

5) Support 2 × 2 × 5 lattice pillar (2580c01)

6) Support 2 × 2 × 2 stand with blind hole (3940a)

7) Support 4 × 4 × 5 stanchion (2680)

8) Support crane stand double (2635)

9) Tower roof 2 × 4 × 4 half cone shaped with roof tiles (35563)

10) Castle turret top 4 × 8 × 2 1/3 (6066)

11) Tower roof 4 × 8 × 6 (6121)

12) Castle turret top 7 × 7 corner (6072)

13) Tower roof 6 × 8 × 9 (33215)

Fences and Stairs

This is some interesting pieces used for detailing, and some you will definitely need to make certain that your minifigs can get to the second, third, or however many floors that you want to make. Unless you want to put in an elevator, but I won't be covering how to do that in this book.

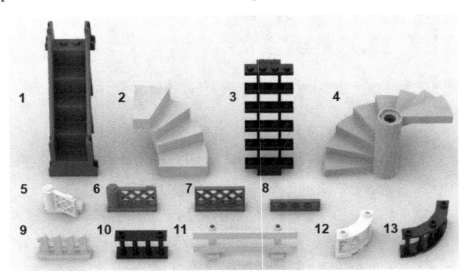

Figure 4-50. *Samples of stairs and fences in LEGO*

1) Stairs 4 × 7 × 9 1/3 straight enclosed (4784)

2) Stairs 6 × 6 × 4 curved (28466)

3) Stairs 7 × 4 × 6 straight open (30134)

4) Stairs spiral steps 16 with support (40243c01)

5) Fence gate 1 × 3 × 2 lattice and base (3358 and 3359)

6) Fence gate 1 × 4 × 2 lattice and base (3186 and 3187)

7) Fence 1 × 4 × 2 lattice (3185)

8) Fence 1 × 4 × 1 lattice (3633)

9) Fence 1 × 4 × 2 paled picket (33303)

10) Fence 1 × 4 × 2 spindled with 2 studs (30055)

11) Fence 1 × 8 × 2 2/3 (6079)

12) Fence 3 × 3 × 2 quarter round ornamental with 2 studs (41823)

13) Fence 4 × 4 × 2 quarter round spindled with 3 studs (21229)

So, this is an example of how to assemble a building with panels, one that could be fit for a second story.

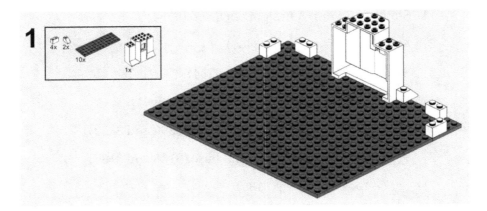

Figure 4-51. *This is where you don't have to use the ten 4 × 12 plates, but you need some kind of foundation of some kind*

You will note how the large panel does overhang off of the initial foundation as shown here.

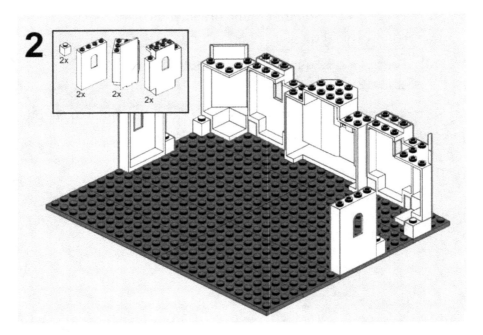

Figure 4-52. *Place on the panels as shown*

You will notice that several of these panels have sections messing down below, and how the bricks put in the following step help secure them. You might notice that the corner sections leave some space, and that is okay.

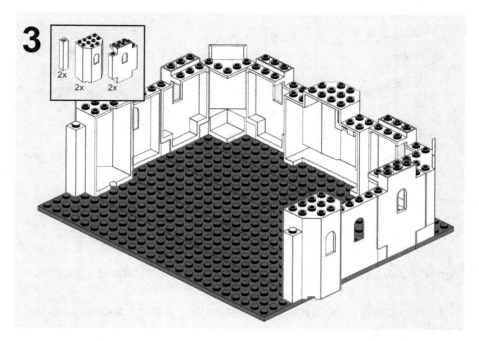

Figure 4-53. *This is a way to create more walls, with panels*

Note in this step the application of a very tall 1 × 1 piece. We actually could have used those for the "slow way" house. Why didn't we? You might want to try building a house with just those and discover why, as they require a lot of securing, which we will do on this building.

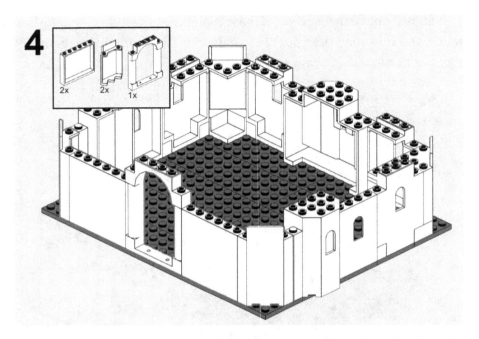

Figure 4-54. *Here is a step to put in some more panels in the front*

I'm not going to bother with a door on this particular formation, but I definitely like the arch on the front. You will notice the 1 × 6 panels and the corners.

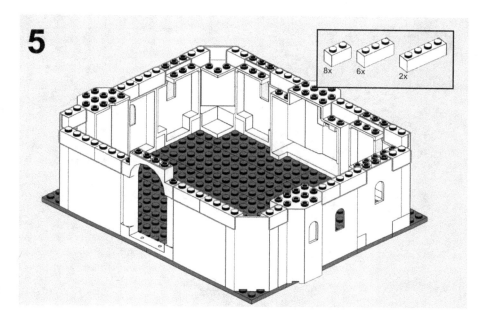

Figure 4-55. *This is where you build up more about this section*

At this point, the parts become much smaller, but you can see how they fit in and how well they will secure the structure as a whole.

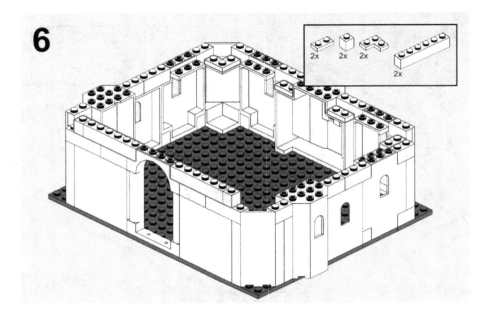

Figure 4-56. *Here, it is about the plates and the blocks*

I have shown in earlier chapters how well plates secure things together, and here, it is going to show how they will really interlock.

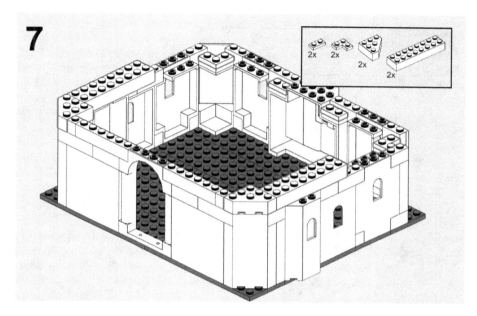

Figure 4-57. *Add on some more plates and blocks on top*

At this point, you are probably seeing how the blocks on top are really holding the structure together as it should be.

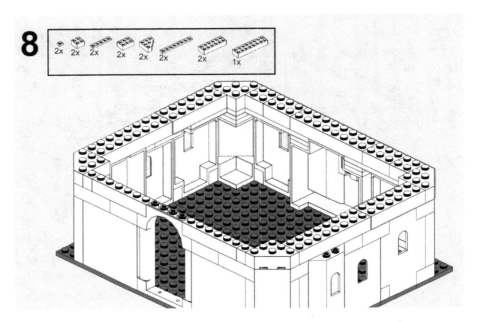

Figure 4-58. *This is where it is time to put in the plates with the blocks on top of that*

Once the plates are on, this is where the blocks really make it secure, and it can be used for another level.

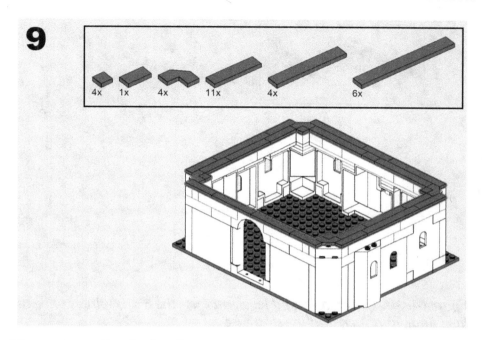

Figure 4-59. *Put in the tiles on top*

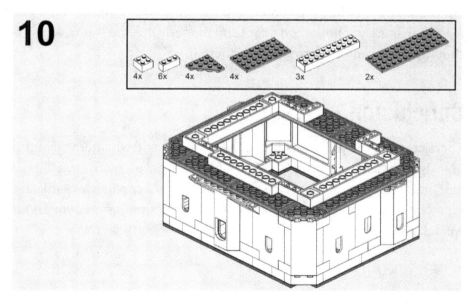

Figure 4-60. *Put on the wedge plates and plates and then the bricks*

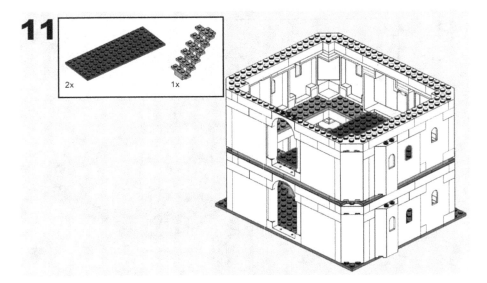

Figure 4-61. *Put on a second level, and use the 6 × 16 plates to be the next floor, and then add the staircase*

Now that you know this, you have the tools necessary to create any kind of house or building you want and make it as tall as you like. I'm going to let you figure out how to do a roof and properly link the staircase, as you should have more than enough skills for that.

Conclusion

There are many ways to construct a LEGO house, and whether you build it quickly with panels or brick by brick, it is best to have a plan, even if it is, at best, crude. Even a sketch on a napkin (or some better paper) is sufficient for laying down a plan to see how much area, in terms of studs, your house will take up.

Once you got your house all set up with all its doors and windows, then it is time to think about how to put a roof on it. I would suggest arranging it so the roof is easily removable, in case you want to alter the interiors. Also, if you want to put a second, third, or how many stories on it, you can have a way of stacking it so it is solid and yet easily accessible.

Why do you need your house to be accessible? Well, you're going to want to fill it with furniture, which is a subject for another chapter.

CHAPTER 5

Smaller Scale: Creating LEGO Furniture and More

A 2010 movie called *Tiny Furniture* is about a woman who is trying to find her sense of purpose after college, and it really has nothing to do with this chapter, other than this is the chapter where I talk about how to create tiny furniture. That is, creating furniture made out of LEGO and designed for the LEGO minifig, which is perfect for filling your house in the last chapter.

LEGO Minifigs

Perhaps I should have taken the time to talk about LEGO minifigs in the last chapter, as it did discuss how to create houses for them. I definitely discussed how a "foot" of a LEGO minifig is equivalent to a 1 × 1 plate. That is enough to give you scale, and the fact that the doors are about 5 or 6 bricks high shows what type of size you are dealing with when building houses.

In writing this book, there were several times where I wonder if I should even mention something, because if you work with LEGO for any given time, you start to realize that there are things that are just base level.

© Mark Rollins 2024
M. Rollins, *Ultimate LEGO Worldbuilding and Architecture*, Maker Innovations Series,
https://doi.org/10.1007/979-8-8688-0521-9_5

Figure 5-1. *Samples of minifigs*

For example, you need to know that a minifig is made up of five parts:

1) Hair/hat

2) Head

3) Backpack or airtank (optional)

4) Arms/waist/midsection

5) Legs

In Chapters 2, 3, and 4, I discussed how to create a base, as well as how to build a LEGO building. The point is to make something as big as you want it to be, assuming you have the pieces to do it with. The next few chapters are going to focus on how to build small, to create things that are made for the minifig scale.

Working Within Your LEGO House Space

I used Chapter 4 to show how to build a house and how to separate sections into rooms, which means, like all home owners, you have to work within your space. Granted, you are more than welcome to create the furniture first and create a house with enough space for just the furniture, as well as any extra space. As someone who lived in a lot of crammed space for about two decades, you learn to value it, but it is difficult when it comes to working in LEGO.

Like I said, one stud is equal to about 1 square foot, it means that you don't have a lot of room to work in a room that is 6 × 6 studs, something that I had in the sample LEGO house. The saddest part is that I realized that there isn't much room for a bathtub and could not put it in at all.

I'm going to just say this: it is more difficult to create something small than something big. When it comes to something big, you can just keep adding on as much as you like. However, if you are building small, you have to use the space you have, and this is where subtlety is key.

Form Follows Function

If you have ever heard the term Bauhaus, then you will usually hear the term of "form follows function." Bauhaus comes from a German art school known as the Staatliches Bauhaus which was famous for a design that did have an individual artistic vision with principles of mass production and emphasis on function. If you Google something such as Bauhaus chair, the emphasis will be simplicity and functionality.

So yes, you will see all kinds of samples of the Bauhaus chair, which will range from the most simple to a little bit more fancy, but nothing overly decorative and not much of an emphasis on comfort. In other words, they live up the reputation of "form follows function," but in the world of LEGO, the same rule can apply.

The LEGO Chair and Table

Take this other chair, as just a few pieces can make this a family heirloom for any minifig.

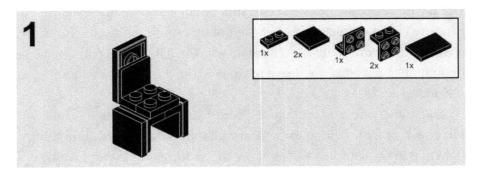

Figure 5-2. *A simple chair construction using some tiles, plates, and brackets*

You will note that there aren't really many studs shown, just those for a minifig blocky butt to sit. The rest is just tiles, and you might notice that this chair will not click into place on a typical LEGO baseplate, unless you make some pieces for it.

Contrast that with this type of chair, which is more of a couch for one.

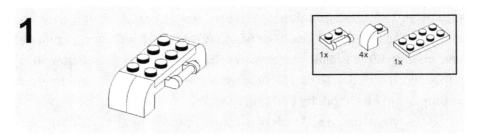

Figure 5-3. *Attach these pieces together as shown as the base of the wider chair*

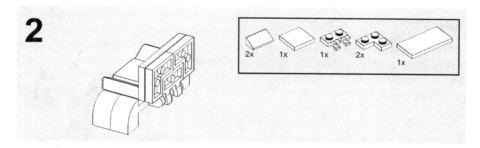

Figure 5-4. *This is where the top portion of the wide chair is finished*

Of course, you can create a couch, if you want. In fact, you could create a double-decker couch.

Okay, enough LEGO movie references, let's talk about this table, and this is about as simple as it gets.

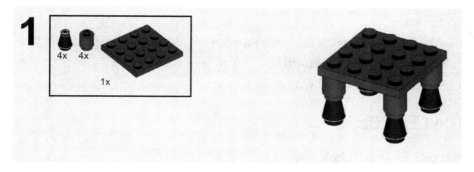

Figure 5-5. *Start with a 4 × 4 plate and add on the round 1 × 1 bricks on the corners, then the 1 × 1 cone bricks*

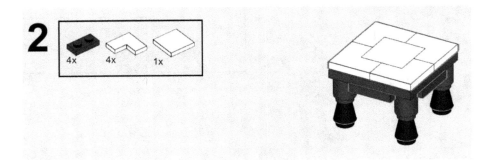

Figure 5-6. *Insert the 2 × 1 plates between the legs and the tile pieces on top*

You will notice that step 1 is simply just making the most basic table with the studs on top. Step 2 is simply just putting in some 1 × 2 plates that don't really add much structurally, but something so simple can add a lot of character.

The same goes with the table and putting the tiles on top. I think I'm going to have to say that putting tiles on something is like putting icing on a cake, it feels like it is the final step.

The LEGO Bed

You will find that it helps when making a LEGO bed.

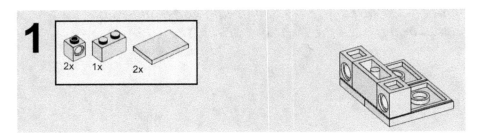

Figure 5-7. *Connect the 1 × 2 brick to the 2 × 3 tiles as shown, with the brick 1 × 1 with hole*

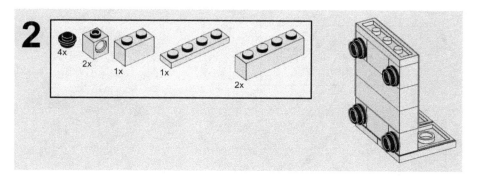

Figure 5-8. *Attach the 1 × 4 bricks on top of step 1, and then place the 1 × 2 Brick with 1 × 1 with through holes atop that. After you cap off the top with the 1 × 4 plate, insert the round 1 × 1 plates*

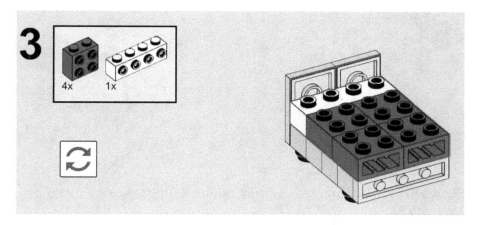

Figure 5-9. *Put on the 1 × 4 brick with studs on the side at top as shown, and then add the 1 × 2 × 1 2/3 with studs on the side*

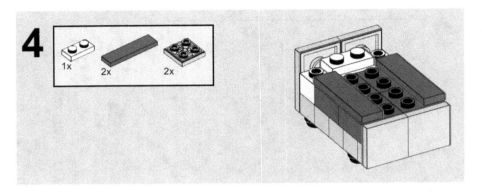

Figure 5-10. *Put on the two modified 2 × 2 inverted tiles. Then put on the 1 × 2 plate and the 1 × 4 tiles*

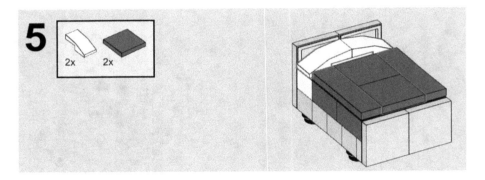

Figure 5-11. *Add on the 2 × 2 tiles, along with the sloped curved 2 × 1 × 2/3*

The LEGO Kitchen Counter

When it comes to the kitchen, it is time to create something necessary for the kitchen, such as a stove, range, sink, a dishwasher, and a cabinet.

Figure 5-12. *Put on the door 1 × 3 × 1 left as shown on the 1 × 8 plate, with a 1 × 1 round bricks, as well as the 1 × 1 brick*

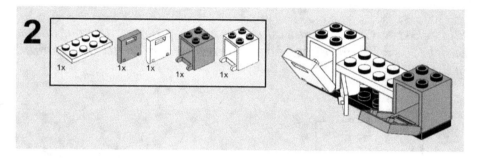

Figure 5-13. *Add on the 1 × 4 plate and then the 2 × 2 × 2 box containers and the door with slots*

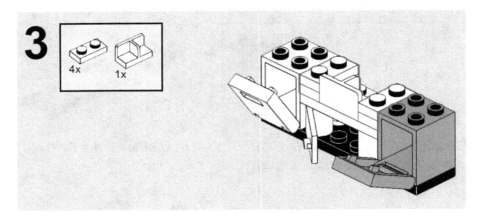

Figure 5-14. *Go ahead and stack on the 1 × 2 plates, and put on the panel 1 × 2 × 1 with rounded corners and center divider in the middle of those*

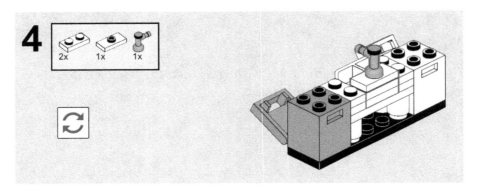

Figure 5-15. *Stack up two 1 × 2 plates, put on the modified plate 1 × 2 with 1 stud, and then put on the tap 1 × 2 with hole*

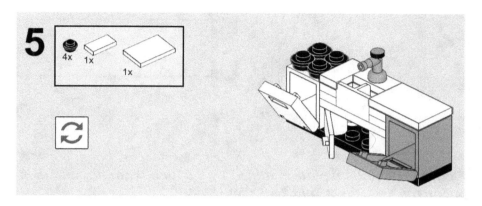

Figure 5-16. *Time to add on the 1 × 2 and 2 × 3 tiles, along with the 1 × 1 round plates on the "stove"*

The LEGO Refrigerator

I have to admit, of all of the appliances that I made for this chapter, this one was the hardest. I tried to make the refrigerator as small as possible, while making it spacious enough to be something that would take up the space it would take up a realistic amount of area in this LEGO minifig world in this LEGO house. I couldn't figure out how to put shelves in it, but I created opening and shutting doors in the main and freezer section.

You might notice that this refrigerator isn't really airtight, in the sense that you can see small cracks in it that would make it not work if you could somehow make it powered with the cold power of a real refrigerator.

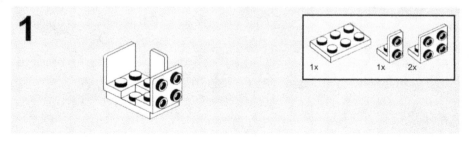

Figure 5-17. *Use a 2 × 3 plate as a base for the bracket 1 × 2 (2 × 2 inverted) and the bracket 1 × 1 (1 × 2 inverted)*

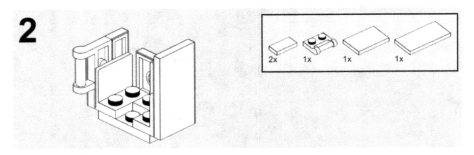

Figure 5-18. *Put on plate modified 1 × 2 with bar handle, and then put on the 1 × 2, 2 × 3, and 2 × 4 tiles*

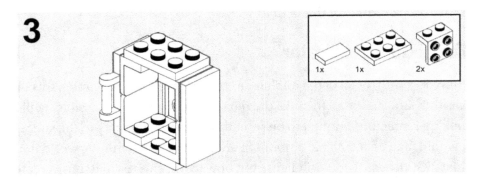

Figure 5-19. *Put on the 1 × 2 (2 × 2) brackets and the 2 × 3 plate and the 1 × 2 tile*

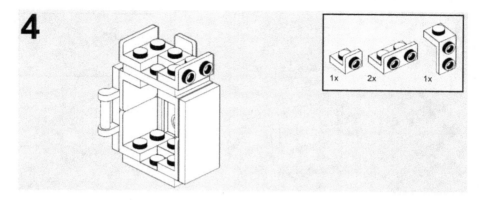

Figure 5-20. *Put on the bracket 1 × 1 (1 × 2) on the bottom of the 2 × 3 plate, and then put on brackets 1 × 2 (1 × 2 inverted) and the bracket 1 × 1 (1 × 1 inverted) on top*

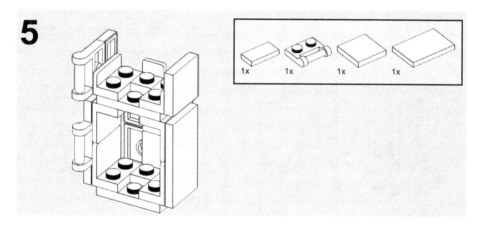

Figure 5-21. *Put on plate modified 1 × 2 with bar handle, and then put on the 1 × 2, 2 × 3, and 2 × 4 tiles*

173

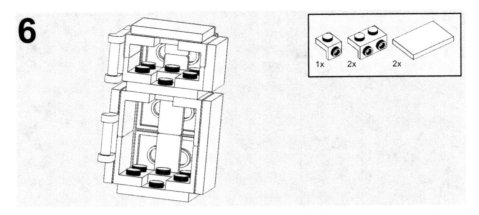

Figure 5-22. *Put on the brackets 1 × 2 (1 × 2 inverted) and the bracket 1 × 1 (1 × 1 inverted). Put on the 2 × 3 tiles on top and on the back*

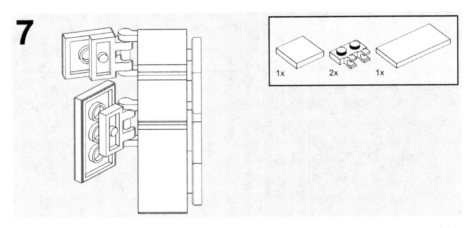

Figure 5-23. *Put on the plates modified 1 × 2 (with two open O clips), and then put on the 2 × 2 and 2 × 4 tiles*

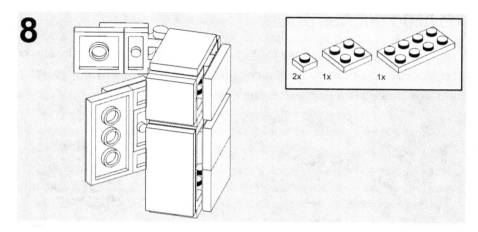

Figure 5-24. *Put on the 2 × 4 and 1 × 1 plates on bottom fridge door and the 2 × 2 plate on the top fridge door*

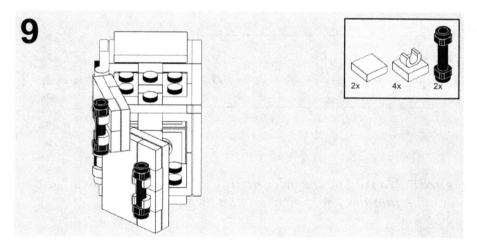

Figure 5-25. *Put on the tile modified 1 × 1 (with open O clip), add the 1 × 1 tiles, and then put on the minifigure weapon hilt smooth extended*

The LEGO Washer/Dryer

Also, it will be good to have a washer and dryer, and I have this one stacked on top of each other, just to conserve space. You could find a way to put them side by side if your house is big enough.

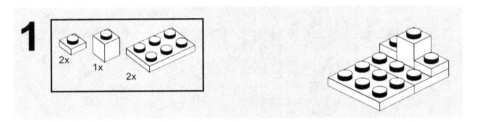

Figure 5-26. *Line up the two 2 × 3 plates, and put on the 1 × 1 plates with the 1 × 1 brick*

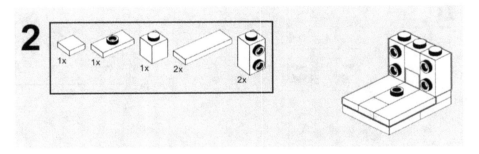

Figure 5-27. *Add on the brick modified 1 × 1 × 1 2/3 with studs on side, with another 1 × 1 brick. Add on the tiles as shown*

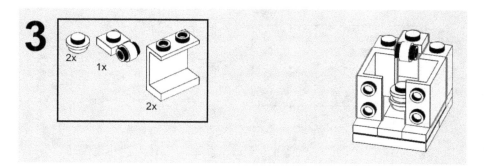

Figure 5-28. *Put on the two 1 × 1 round plates, with the two 1 × 2 × 2 panels. Put on the modified plate 1 × 1 with light attachment*

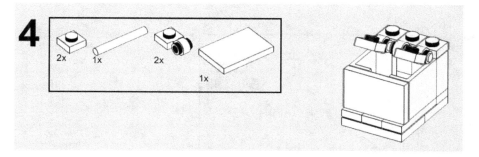

Figure 5-29. *Slide the 3 M bar through the 1 × 1 modified plate with light attachment from the last step, and then slide on the other two modified plates on this step. Don't forget to add on the 2 × 3 tile*

177

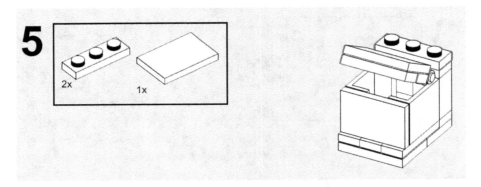

Figure 5-30. *Put on the 2 × 3 tile on the modified tiles, and then put on the 1 × 3 plate*

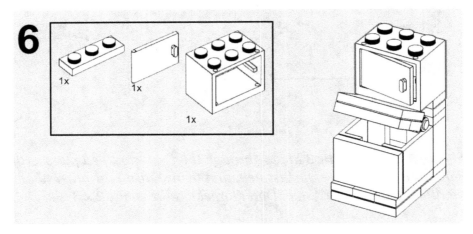

Figure 5-31. *Once you put on the 1 × 3 plate, put on the 2 × 3 × 2 container cupboard on top*

And of course, what home isn't complete without a toilet? I believe that I have been promising this one in previous chapters, so here it is.

The LEGO Toilet

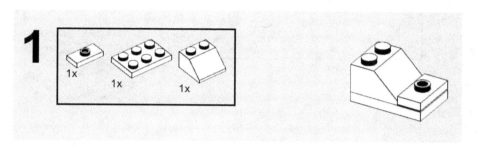

Figure 5-32. *Put on the modified tile with center stud on the 2 × 3 tile, with the slope 45 2 × 2*

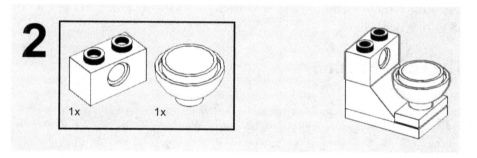

Figure 5-33. *Put on the 1 × 2 block with a through hole and brick round 2 × 2 dome bottom*

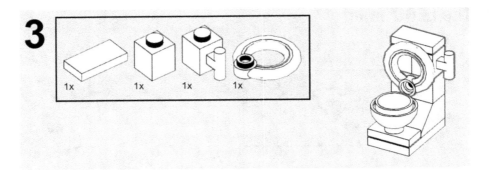

Figure 5-34. *Go ahead and put on the minifigure utensil flotation ring and the 1 × 1 brick. Then use the 1 × 1 modified brick with bar handle, with the 1 × 2 tile*

Oh, and if you are going to make a toilet, then you are going to need a tub, so here is a tub here.

The LEGO Bathtub

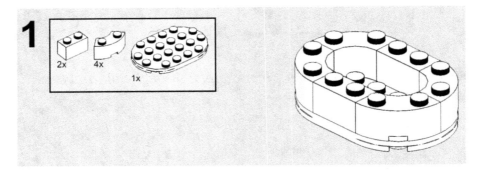

Figure 5-35. *Use the round 4 × 6 oval as a base, and then use the round corner 2 × 2 blocks, with the 1 × 2 blocks to fill it in*

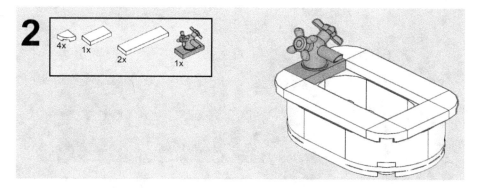

Figure 5-36. *Put on this faucet piece, and then use the tiles to fill in the corners*

Now that you have a lot of furniture, take the time to put them in your house. You will find that some of it will fit on the studs of the floor, but some will not. I couldn't fit in the tub in my first home design, and so I redesigned my home around it.

Figure 5-37. *The furniture in the LEGO house*

Conclusion

When it comes to making furniture for LEGO houses, or homes for LEGO minifigs, it is important to know the amount of space that you have to work with. LEGO pieces can often take up a lot of space, at least a stud, so it is difficult to create something that is representative of a thing with minute details.

Some of the furniture isn't going to be functional, like how the bed doesn't really have sheets that a LEGO minifig can tuck themselves in. Still, it adds a depth of realism to a living space in a LEGO minifig, which is an important detail in really bringing any LEGO creation to life.

We'll talk more creating details on LEGO projects that are more "outdoor" rather than indoor in later chapters, starting with the automobile.

CHAPTER 6

Cars and Trains, Designing Anything with Wheels in LEGO

Well, when I designed the base for a LEGO mass creation in Chapters 2 and 3, I wanted to make roads that had lanes with traffic flowing in both directions, which means that I was going to need a lot of space to make it work. Now, it is time to make vehicles that will work as well.

The vehicles that I will demonstrate in this chapter are definitely made for minifigs, so they will be small and have very little features. If you're lucky, you're going to be able to open doors, but sliding the characters in and out might be impossible to do if you were an actual LEGO minifig.

I mean, as an example, there is a LEGO Batmobile that has a cool convertible top so the Caped Crusader can get quickly and conveniently in and out, but there is a distinct lack of room inside for Robin.

When I designed the roads, I made them so they are about ten studs wide, that means you could build your cars eight studs wide and have a good clearance of about one stud on each side, but that might still not be playing it safe. If we go by one stud equals about one foot, then cars that pass each other with one foot of clearance isn't very safe now, is it?

© Mark Rollins 2024
M. Rollins, *Ultimate LEGO Worldbuilding and Architecture*, Maker Innovations Series, https://doi.org/10.1007/979-8-8688-0521-9_6

Basic LEGO Techniques for Vehicle Constructions

So, it is better to be safe and go for about six studs wide, with a little bit of overhang on each side. As I discussed in the Chapters 4 and 5, space becomes crucial when designing a living space, and this is important in developing the exterior and interior of a car.

However, space gets limited inside a LEGO car very quickly if you are seating two LEGO minifigs next to each other. Considering that LEGO minifigs are practically four studs wide (two at the waist, plus another two if you count the arms), this can result in some seriously cramped quarters.

Note that most cars are cramped to begin with. If you really think about it, there isn't a lot of space for arms and legs, and current LEGO minifigs do not bend at the knee, making it more difficult in a LEGO automobile setting. Fortunately, there are always workarounds. I've seen some LEGO builders remove the legs entirely from the minifigs, and some will just remove the body altogether and just put in the head (seriously). All I can say is, if you need the space, then you need the space.

Sadly, there won't be a lot of features on these minifig cars, as they are designed only with wheels. You won't be able to steer them like LEGO Technic cars, or take control, as they are too small in scale for details such as that. You can read my other LEGO Technic book for something like that if making cars on a bigger scale is for you. I will be using some techniques to create the frames, which is the most difficult part.

When it comes to building cars, LEGO actually has design frames for this. In fact, they have all kinds of fenders and such, but I would rather focus on building as much from scratch as possible, note that you can't find some of these frames on Bricklink or other websites devoted to LEGO sales.

When it comes to cars, most experts agree that you should just go out and purchase a set with a car, build the car, and see what you can learn from it. After all, this is the best way to learn is to imitate and expand, or find other models on Rebrickable. By the way, this is the first time that I have mentioned Rebrickable (`https://rebrickable.com/`), a site devoted to making new models out of existing LEGO sets.

Oh, you should also know that LEGO also makes many parts that are devoted to making cars, and here are some examples:

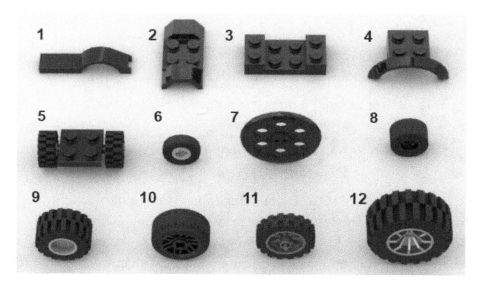

Figure 6-1. *Samples of LEGO pieces made specifically for cars*

1) Vehicle, mudguard 1 × 4 ½ (50947)

2) Vehicle, mudguard 2 × 4 with arch smooth (3787)

3) Vehicle, mudguard 2 × 4 with arch studded (3788)

4) Vehicle, mudguard 4 × 2 ½ × 1 with arch round (98282)

5) Plate, modified 2 × 2 with red wheels with black tires 15 mm × 6 mm (122c01assy2)

6) Technic bush 1/2 smooth with black tire 14 mm × 4mm smooth small (4265cc01)

7) Technic wedge belt wheel with black technic wedge belt wheel tire (4185c01)

8) Wheel 8 mm × 9 mm for slicks, hole notched for wheels holder pin (74967c01)

9) Wheel 11 mm × 12 mm hole round for wheels holder pin with black tire (6014ac01)

10) Wheel 14mm × 9.9 mm with center groove fake bolts and 6 double spokes (11208c01)

11) Wheel 15 mm × 6 mm city motorcycle with black tire 21 mm × 6 mm (50862c01)

12) Wheel 18 mm × 14 mm spoked with black tire 20.4 × 14 offset tread (51377c02)

Also, most of the LEGO car building experts love to start building the front and backs of their vehicle, and once they got that set up, they will fill it in on the sides. It is similar to how I design LEGO Technic vehicles, where I figure out how I want to do the steering and engine and then work around that to the frame. Since I happen to be building a bigger version of the Dodge Charger SXT for my LEGO Technic book, I think I'm going to do a demonstration of how to do that in minifig scale.

I looked at my local car dealership and found some pics of the Dodge Charger SXT that I could use as reference.

Figure 6-2. *Pictures of the Dodge Charger SXT taken for reference of the front, back, and side*

I recommend that if you want to create a certain type of automobile, you should take pics of the actual car or find them on the Internet.

Dodge Charger SXT

Okay, since I am writing two books about LEGO, I really wanted to give readers a sample of what types of vehicles that you can actually make in LEGO. It is pretty difficult when the subject is very curvaceous, but it can be done. I show how to do a Dodge Charger SXT in LEGO Technic, and now I'm going to show how to do it in LEGO minifig.

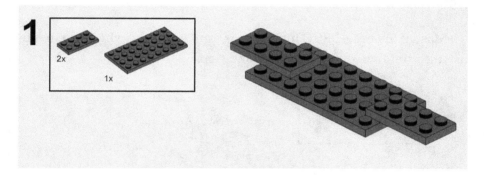

Figure 6-3. *Put the 2 × 4 plates on the 4 × 8 plates as shown*

This is where the base of the Dodge Charger comes in.

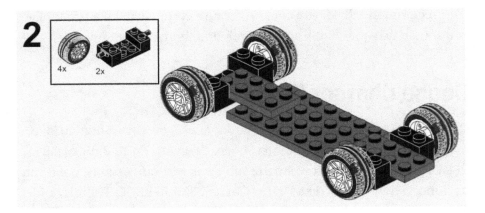

Figure 6-4. *Put on the wheels on the 2 × 4 plates as shown*

Most of the time, LEGO instructions want to put the wheels on in the last time, but I'm doing it in the second step.

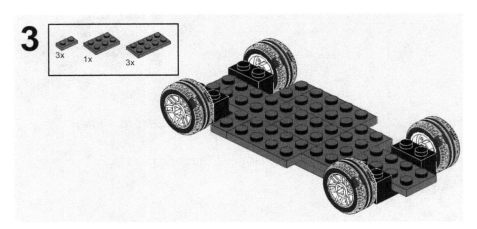

Figure 6-5. *Put on the plates as shown*

Now that the base and wheels are set, it is time to widen it for the buildup.

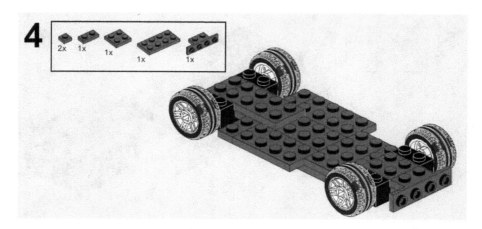

Figure 6-6. *Time to put on more plates, as well as the bracket that will be in the back of the Dodge Charger*

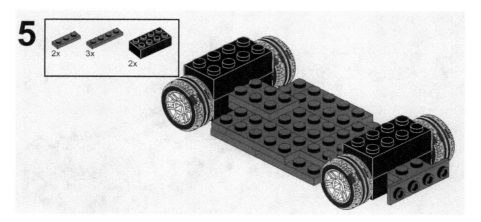

Figure 6-7. *Add on the 2 × 4 bricks, and the plates go on the side*

Since this car is only six bricks wide, this is where we can add the side.

189

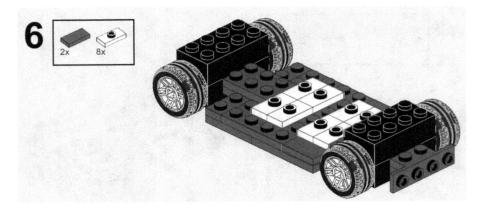

Figure 6-8. *In addition to the 1 × 2 tiles, it is time to put on the modified plates*

This is where the minifigs will sit, and you can actually fit four of them in this tiny space.

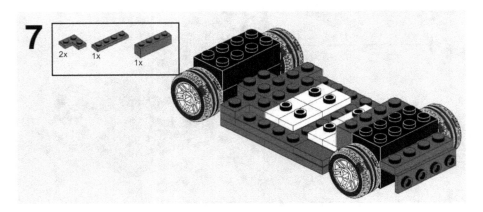

Figure 6-9. *Put on the plates as shown, along with the 1 × 4 brick*

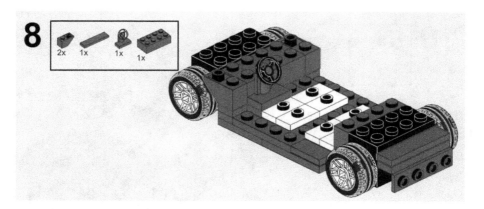

Figure 6-10. *Put in the reverse slopes as well the 2 × 4 brick. The steering wheel is put in the driver's seat and the 1 × 4 tile*

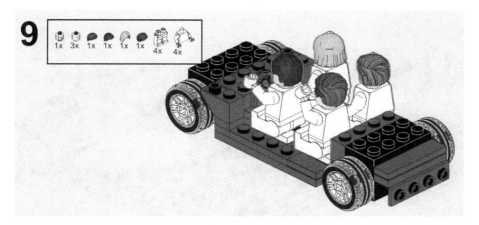

Figure 6-11. *Time to put in the minifigs so their legs are the modified tiles*

You will note that in order to fit in the minifigs, you will have to adjust their arms so they are not abreast of each other.

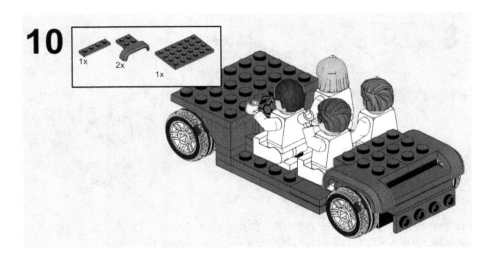

Figure 6-12. *Put on the tops over the wheels*

Figure 6-13. *Time to put on the brackets and the plates*

Figure 6-14. *So, put on the plates and the modified bricks as shown*

Figure 6-15. *Time to put on the headlights and help complete the front of the car*

Figure 6-16. *Another step to creating the front of the car*

Figure 6-17. *Time to put on the tiles on here*

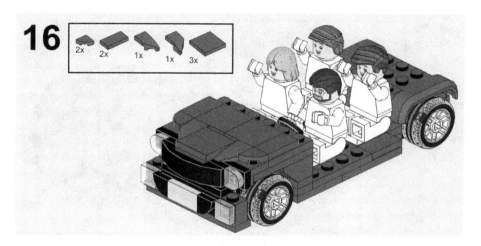

Figure 6-18. *Time to put on the hood for the car with these tiles*

Figure 6-19. *Time to focus on the back of the Dodge Charger*

Figure 6-20. *Time to put on the truck on this, or at least start it*

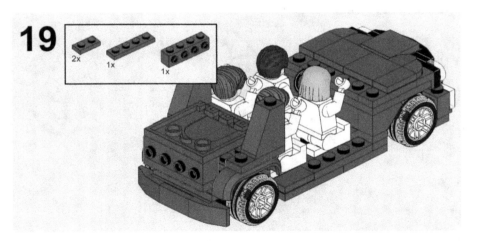

Figure 6-21. *Another time to build up the back of the Dodge Charger SXT*

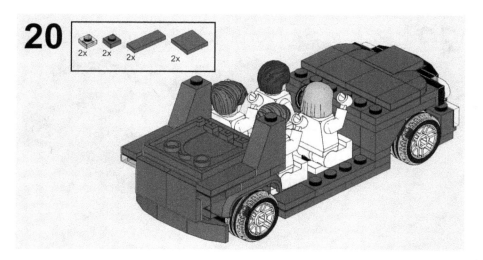

Figure 6-22. *This is another time to build up the back of the car*

Figure 6-23. *Time to add on the taillights*

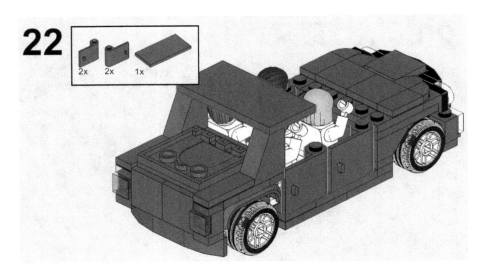

Figure 6-24. *Put on the doors at part of the roof*

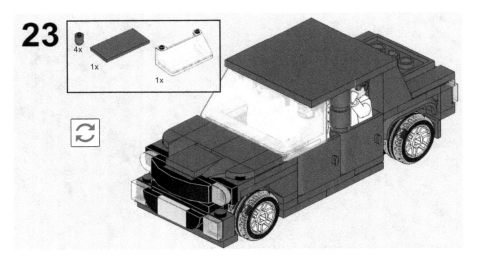

Figure 6-25. *Once the glass and the round bricks with the roof*

A Brief Section on Trains

I believe that I promised that I would touch on trains here, and if you are a big LEGO train fan, you are probably going to be disappointed. The fact is that most LEGO train sets come with sets of instructions, and I actually didn't think there was much I could add to them in this chapter.

If you want to construct a certain type of train that LEGO does not make, I would suggest applying the same principles to building cars, only find the proper wheels and parts necessary for making trains.

After that, it just becomes a challenge of getting your tracks and putting them where you want. Unfortunately, I don't think the foundational base that I designed in Chapters 2 and 3 could accommodate a train, but I could be wrong.

Honestly, trains and model railroading is such a complicated topic. I could probably write a book on that. Now that I am writing this, I'm wondering if I should. Hmm…for now, I'd better get to the conclusion.

Conclusion

When it comes to creating LEGO vehicles, it isn't just about putting wheels on something and calling it good. After all, I think we all know that there is a lot of engineering put in a real car, and you are going to have to put a lot of construction skills to create a vehicle that can hold just two drivers.

It is possible to use these pre-made car frames to create a vehicle, but it is a meticulous process of figuring out how to fit in the LEGO minifigs. That, and figuring out how to imitate the shape of the car frame that you are trying to replicate.

I will recommend getting as many pictures as possible of the car that you are attempting to replicate in minifig scale and use smaller scale building techniques to get it to look as much like the vehicle as possible.

From there, you can start laying down the pieces that you need for a road, because where these LEGO cars are going, they are going to need roads. Or tracks, if you are building a train.

Unless, you want to build an airplane or helicopter, which is the subject of the next chapter, not to mention boats.

CHAPTER 7

LEGO Planes, Helicopters, and Boats

I spent a lot of time covering how to make a LEGO car, and several of these principles can be used in creating a LEGO plane. Although they will not actually fly, LEGO planes have come a long way since their introduction in 1961. Back then, it was a bunch of bricks put together that had a resemblance of an airplane shape and would assuredly fly like a brick.

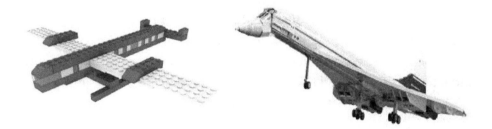

Figure 7-1. *LEGO set 311-4, the company's first foray into airplanes, followed by the Concorde set 10318*

When it comes to planes, most of the first official models were stacking plates together to achieve a greater sense of detail in more of a LEGO Architecture type build, such as this model set of 10318, the Concorde. There was a 1977 model created with minifigs that kind of worked with

© Mark Rollins 2024
M. Rollins, *Ultimate LEGO Worldbuilding and Architecture*, Maker Innovations Series,
https://doi.org/10.1007/979-8-8688-0521-9_7

set 712, but back then, the minifigs were the ones that had stubs for arms and stiff legs. It took all the way until 1985 before a city set, simply called Airport, had a plane that a minifig could be a pilot for.

Figure 7-2. *Set 712 (left) in 1977 and then an improvement with set 6392 in 1985*

By the 2000s, the airplane sets were getting more and more advanced, and part of that was the creation of very large pre-fab pieces that represented the cockpit, fuselage, wings, and much more. As I mentioned before, you could build a plane with these pieces, and I'll go into more detail on this later, because the kits you can buy from will show you how to do that, and all that is required is to follow the instructions.

The key in creating planes is to make a cockpit that can house a pilot and have wings and a tail that would accommodate flight. You are also going to need some method of propulsion, whether it be a propeller or jet engine. Oh, and you are going to need some landing gear as well or at least some pontoons if you are making one of those seaplanes, but I will leave that up to you.

While much of this chapter will show how to make a typical LEGO plane that is minifig scale, I do give instructions on how to make a rudimentary helicopter. I also devote a little time on boats, but not much, as I have to admit that much of the LEGO worlds I talk about here don't really have much water.

Constructing Planes

For this next demonstration, I decided to do a small plane, and I just decided to Google "most popular small plane" and ended up with the Cessna 172 Skyhawk. After looking at pics of this very small plane (similar to building techniques of an automobile in Chapter 6), I definitely thought: "oh yeah, this is it, I want to build this." In fact, I thought it was so good to be true that I immediately went only doing a search for LEGO Cessna 172 just to make certain LEGO hadn't already done an official model already.

To my surprise, they hadn't, but I was able to find a few LEGO imitators that had. Also, there will always be Rebrickable and other ideas that you can find online, because, let's face it, LEGO has a following of builders that is unparalleled.

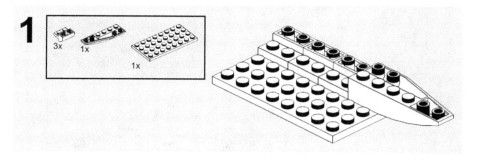

Figure 7-3. *Put down the 4 × 8 plate, and then add on the three slope curved 2 × 2 as well as the wedge 6 × 2 inverted left*

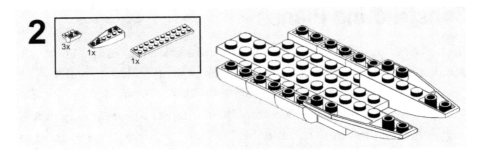

Figure 7-4. *Put down the 2 × 10 plate on the 4 × 8 plate, and then add on the other parts like the slope curved 2 × 2 and the wedge 6 × 2 inverted right so the creation is symmetrical*

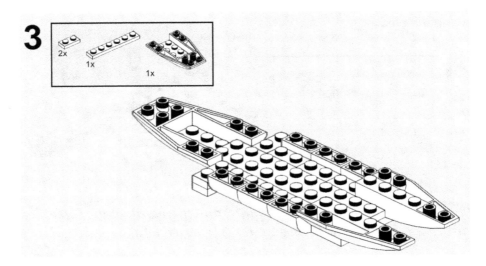

Figure 7-5. *Put on the 1 × 6 plate and the 2 × 1 plates, adding on the wedge 6 × 4 triple inverted curved*

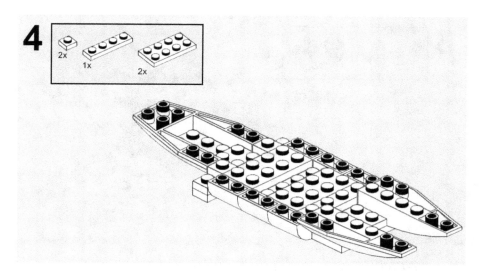

Figure 7-6. *Put on the 2 × 4 plates, the 1 × 4 plate, and the 1 × 1 plates as shown*

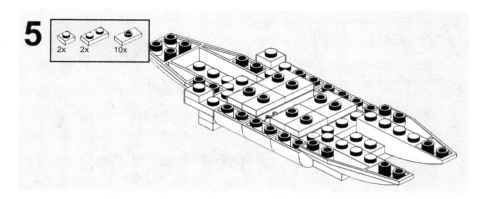

Figure 7-7. *Put on the 1 × 2 plates, along with the modified plates 1 × 2 with stud*

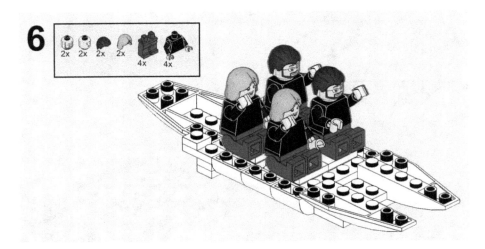

Figure 7-8. *It's time to put in the minifigs. You could put them in later, but it often is easier to put in the minifigs and build around them, especially in a case where the minifigs are in close quarters*

Figure 7-9. *Put in the 2 × 2 plates in front of the minifigs to allow the modified brick 1 × 4 with channel, the two 1 × 1 bricks, the two hinge bricks 1 × 2. Put on the wedge 4 × 2 left and the wedge 4 × 2 right*

Figure 7-10. *Put on the two 1 × 2 bricks on the sides, the 1 × 2 brick with stud on the side, and the two modified bricks with headlight; then add on the wedge 4 × 2 left and wedge 4 × 2 right. Put on the two hinge cylinders 1 × 2 locking with axle hole with the angles as shown*

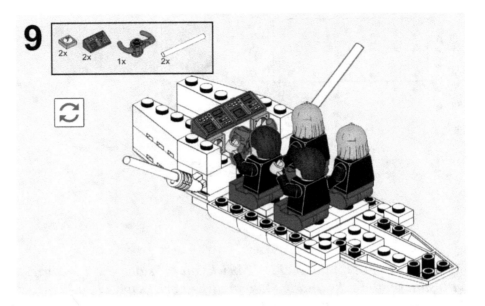

Figure 7-11. *Put on a steering wheel, with the two tiles 1 x 1 with white and red gauge, along with the two slope 30 1 × 2 × 2/3 with pattern. Insert the 4M bars here*

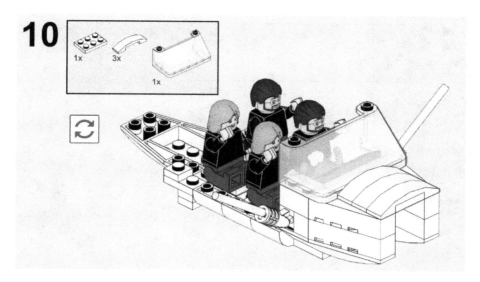

Figure 7-12. *Put on the windscreen 3 × 6 × 2 and the three slope curved 4 × 1 × 2/3 double, and put a 2 × 3 plate under them*

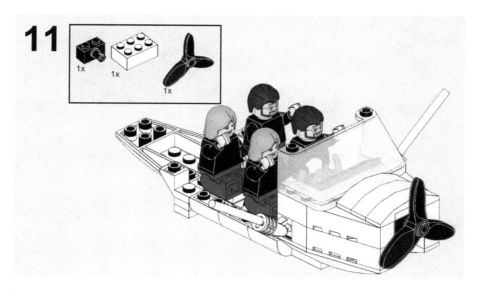

Figure 7-13. *Underneath the last step, put on the 2 × 3 brick, then the brick modified 1 × 2 with peg, and the propeller 3 blade 5.5 diameter*

Figure 7-14. *Much of this step takes place in front of the plane with the slope inverted 33 3 × 2 with flat bottom and the slope inverted 45 2 × 2 here. Add on the brick 2 × 2 and plate 1 × 2, and in the back, put on the 2 × 2 plate*

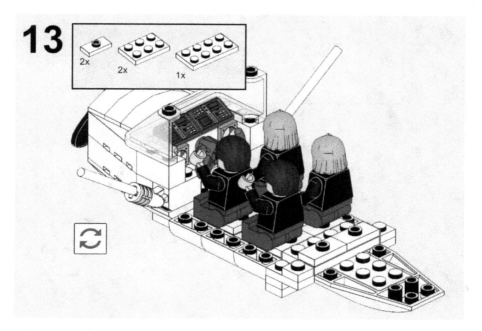

Figure 7-15. *Put the 2 × 3 plates in the wedge 6 × 4 triple inverted curved, and stack the 2 × 4 plate as shown, with the plate modified 1 × 2 with stud*

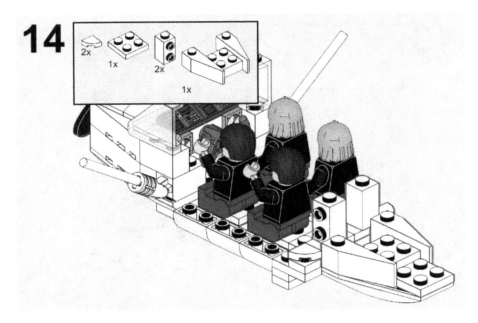

Figure 7-16. *Put on the wedge 3 1/2 × 4 without stud notches, and then put on the 2 × 2 plate. Put on the two tiles round 1 × 1 quarter and the two brick modified 1 × 1 × 1 2/3 with studs on the side*

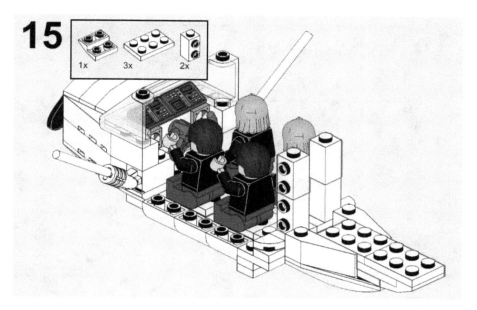

Figure 7-17. *Put on the two 2 × 3 plates on top, with the slope curved 2 × 2 × 2/3 inverted on bottom. Stack on the brick modified 1 × 1 × 1 2/3 with studs on the side*

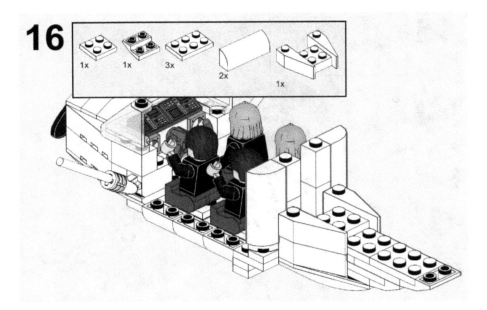

Figure 7-18. *Put on the 2 × 2 plate, the slope curved 2 × 2 × 2/3 inverted on bottom, the wedge 3 1/2 × 4, the three 2 × 3 plates, and the slope curved 1 × 4 × 1 1/3*

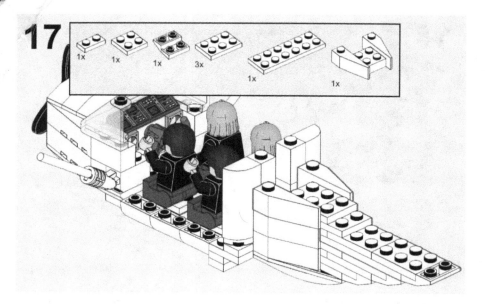

Figure 7-19. *Put on the 2 × 6 plate, the 2 × 3 plates, the 2 × 2 plate, and the 1 × 2 plate. Put on the wedge 3 1/2 × 4 and the slope curved 2 × 2 × 2/3 inverted*

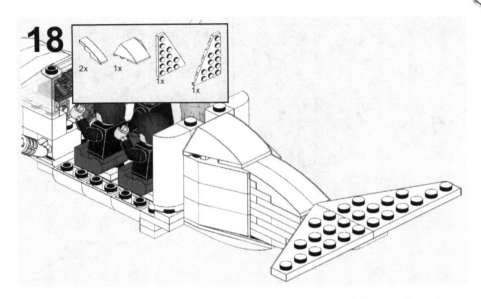

Figure 7-20. *Put on the wedge plate 6 × 4 right and the wedge plate 6 × 4 left. Put on the slope curved 4 × 1 and the wedge 4 × 3 triple curved no studs*

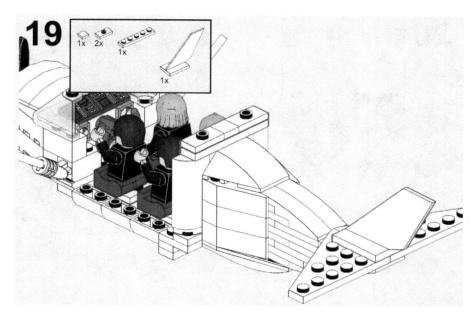

Figure 7-21. *Put on the 1 × 5 plate as shown with the 1 × 2 modified bricks with stud and the 1 × 1 tile. Put the tail shuttle on the end*

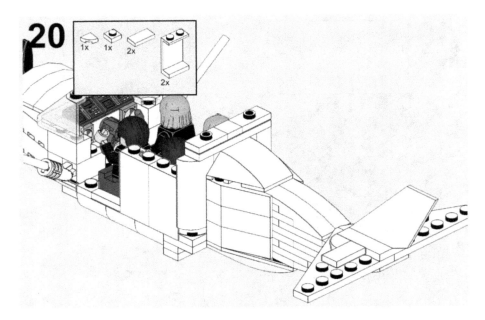

Figure 7-22. *Put a 1 × 1 plate in front with the 1 × 2 tile, and then put on the panel 1 × 2 × 3. Then put the 1 × 2 tile and tile round 1 × 1 quarter near the tail shuttle*

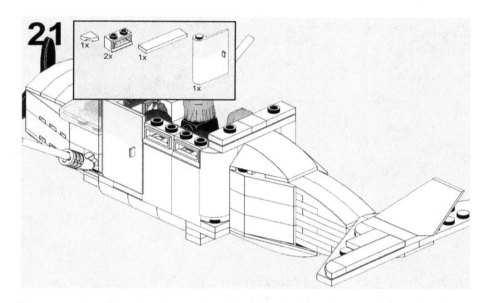

Figure 7-23. *Put the door 1 × 3 × 4 left with window, along with the window 1 × 2 × 1. Then put the 1 × 4 tile and tile round 1 × 1 quarter near the tail shuttle*

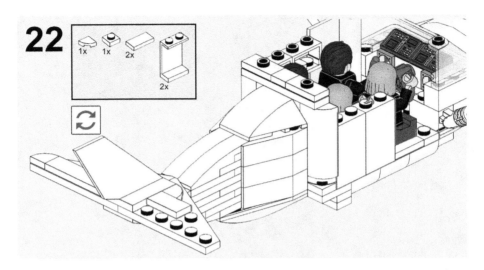

Figure 7-24. Put a 1 × 1 plate in front with the 1 × 2 tile, and then put on the panel 1 × 2 × 3. Then put the 1 × 2 tile and tile round 1 × 1 quarter

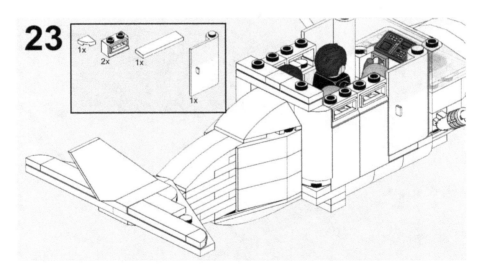

Figure 7-25. Put the door 1 × 3 × 4 right with window, along with the window 1 × 2 × 1. Then put the 1 × 4 tile and tile round 1 × 1 quarter near the tail shuttle

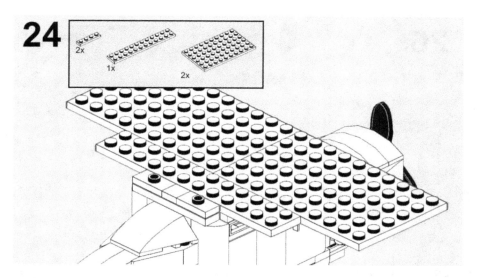

Figure 7-26. *Use the 1 × 4 plates on the 1 × 2 × 1 windows, and then cap off the roof with the two 6 × 10 plates and the 2 × 12 plate*

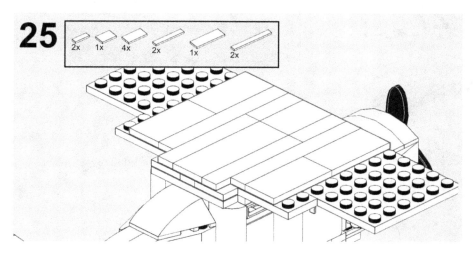

Figure 7-27. *Put all the tiles on top, like the 1 × 3, 1 × 6, and 1 × 8, not to mention the 2 × 3, 2 × 4, and 2 × 6 tiles*

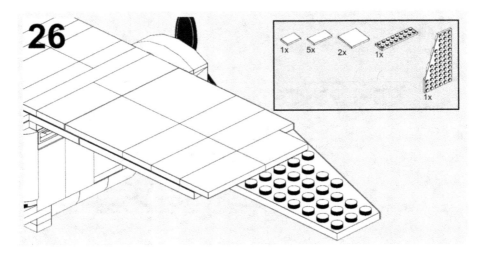

Figure 7-28. *Put on the many tiles like the 2 × 3, 2 × 4, and 4 × 4, and then put on the 2 × 8 plate and the wedge plate 12 × 6 left*

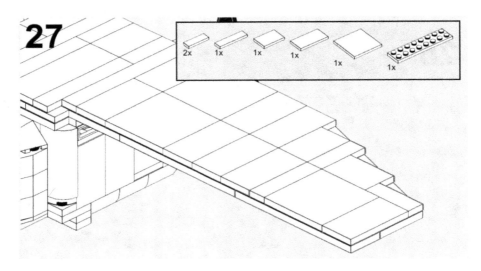

Figure 7-29. *Put on the tiles like the 1 × 3, 1 × 4, 2 × 3, 2 × 4, and 4 × 4. The 2 × 8 plate holds it in place*

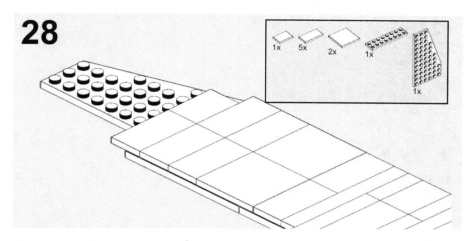

Figure 7-30. *Put on the many tiles like the 2 × 3, 2 × 4, and 4 × 4, and then put on the 2 × 8 plate and the wedge plate 12 × 6 right*

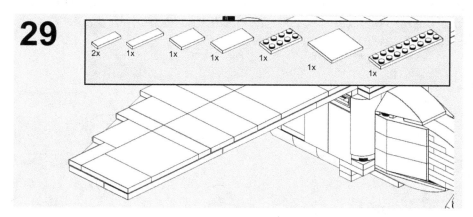

Figure 7-31. *Put on the tiles like the 1 × 3, 1 × 4, 2 × 3, 2 × 4, and 4 × 4. The 2 × 8 plate holds it in place. Put the 2 × 4 plate on the bottom as shown*

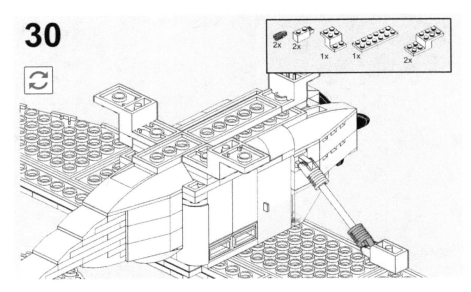

Figure 7-32. *Put on the bracket 3 × 2 × 1 1/3 with bottom stud holder and the two brackets 5 × 2 × 1 1/3 with 2 holes. Put on the 2 × 6 plate and the hinge brick 1 × 2 and hinge cylinder 1 × 2*

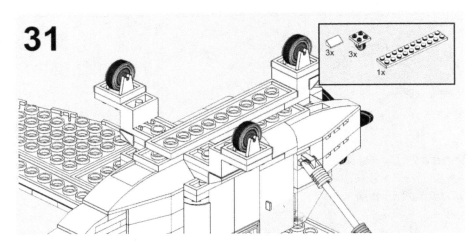

Figure 7-33. *Put on the three plates modified 2 × 2 with wheel on the bottom as shown. Put the three slope 30 1 × 2 × 2/3 on the brackets, and put on the 2 × 10 plate as shown*

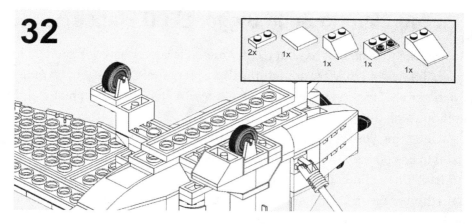

Figure 7-34. *Use the slope 45 2 × 2, the slope 33 3 × 2, and tile 2 × 2 on top of the wheel. Use the slope 45 2 × 2 with the two 1 × 2 tiles on the bottom*

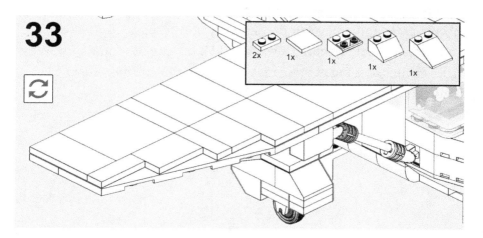

Figure 7-35. *Use the slope 45 2 × 2, the slope 33 3 × 2, and tile 2 × 2 on top of the wheel. Use the slope 45 2 × 2 with the two 1 × 2 tiles on the bottom*

So, You Want to Build Bigger LEGO Planes?

So, yes, the Cessna that has been constructed is very, very cool, but you might be striving to make something like a jet plane! Okay, if you want to do that, then I highly suggest looking at the dimensions of a jet plane and creating a bit of a plan for your plane.

One thing you will notice on any passenger plane is how there would need to be spots for three passengers on each side, and you probably noticed how difficult it is to sit two LEGO figures sitting side by side. I used a method of those modified bricks, and they will fit in an area that is about eight studs wide, which is enclosed.

You realize that making a plane like this would require a lot of space, about x studs on each side, with a narrow aisle that could be two studs wide, barely accommodating the drink and snack cart. I'm going to leave that up to you (hence the x in the last sentence), not to mention creating a cockpit, and another level underneath for storing luggage.

I suppose that you could always build it the easy way, and by the easy way, I mean use some of these massive pieces that are in some LEGO plane sets.

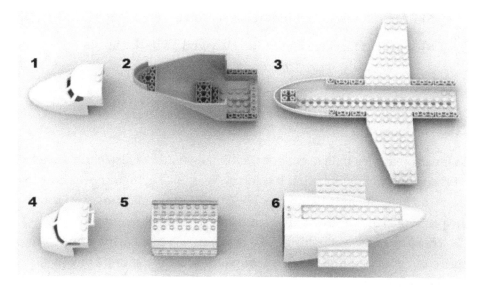

Figure 7-36. *Samples of pieces designed to make building LEGO airplanes much easier*

Like all sample piece illustrations that are in this book, this is not meant to be an exhaustive list. This is what these are, in case you want to get them on BrickLink, eBay, or other LEGO venues.

1) Aircraft fuselage forward top curved 6 × 10 × 4 with 5 window panes (18907)

2) Aircraft fuselage aft section curve bottom 8 × 16 with 2 holes (67244)

3) Aircraft fuselage forward bottom curved 6 × 24 × 1 1/3 with 4 × 21 recessed center and 12 × 6 wings, 20 holes (67138)

4) Aircraft fuselage forward top curved 6 × 6 with bar handle and 3 pin hole (29114)

5)   Aircraft fuselage middle angular top 6 × 8 × 4 (42604)

6)   Aircraft fuselage aft section curved with dark bluish gray base (54702c02)

Helicopters

As far as creating a helicopter goes, I will tell you that I also can't make it fly. Again, I'm guessing that it is too dangerous. I actually cover how to create a LEGO Technic helicopter in my LEGO Technic book, and some of the principles of non-flight apply, but at least there is a motor!

These are very basic things, like how you will need at least one rotor above the pilot and then another side rotor. Here is a sample of how to build one using a principle of reverse engineering.

Before you criticize me, I will tell you that yes, I am going to just take the basic structure of the Cessna and turn it into a helicopter. This is a good way to learn how to do LEGO, and it is a way that I have been building with LEGO for decades. That is, you look at a model that has already been completed and find ways to use the basic structure to build something different, even if it is only slightly.

So, if you want to build a helicopter, here's what you can do. Build everything in the Cessna, but stop at step 23. I even changed the color of the parts, so it looks a little bit different in the plans.

We are going to change step 11. We're going to remove the propeller (4617) and the modified brick 1 × 2 with peg (2458) and just replace that modified brick with a regular brick 1 × 2 (3004). We will also remove the two hinge cylinder 1 × 2 (30553) pieces from step 8 and the 4M bar (30374) pieces from step 9. We can also remove the hinge brick 1 × 2 (30364) and replace it with a regular brick 1 × 2 (3004).

Now, let's go to the back of the tail of the plane. We are going to remove the tail shuttle piece (6239), as well as the wedge plates 6 × 4 (48205 and 48208) and the many tiles (25269, 3069, and 2431).

From this, we then have a new step 23 to start at, which is essentially just the part where the pilots and passengers fit. From there, you can turn this Cessna body into a helicopter. If only it were that easy in real life.

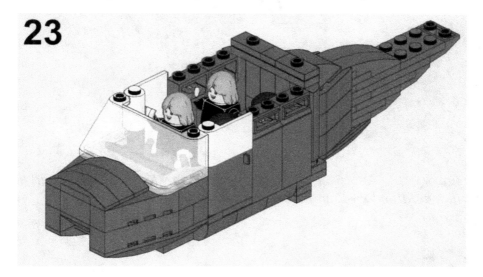

Figure 7-37. *Once you have removed the parts from the previous steps of the Cessna, as described above, this is the start of your helicopter*

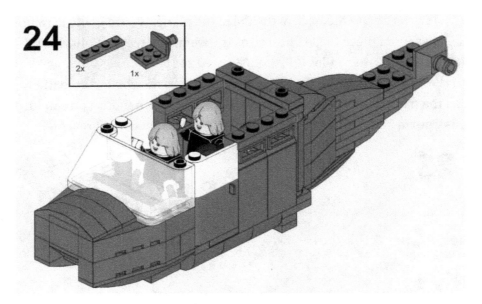

Figure 7-38. *Apply the 1 × 4 plates on the windows, and then add the plate modified 2 × 2 with helicopter tail rotor holder*

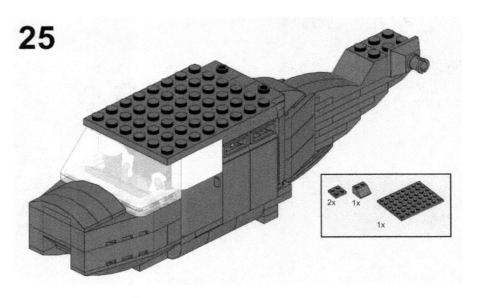

Figure 7-39. *Top off the roof with a 6 × 8 plate, and put two 2 × 2 plates atop the tail rotor holder, and put the slope 45 2 × 2 there as well*

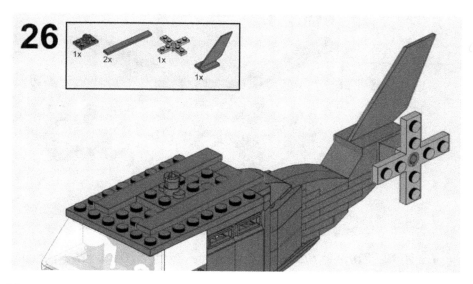

Figure 7-40. *Put on the two 1 × 8 tiles on top, with the plate modified 2 × 3 with helicopter rotor holder. Use a tail shuttle and propeller 4 blade 5 diameter 5 × 5 with center hole*

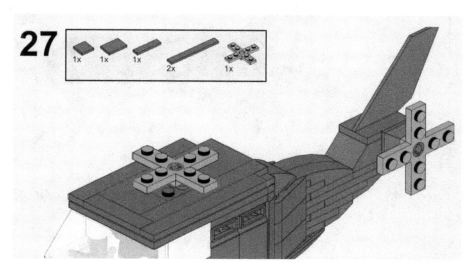

Figure 7-41. *Time to put on tiles like the two 1 × 8, the 1 × 4, the 2 × 2, and the 2 × 3. Time to put on the propeller 4 blade 5 diameter 5 × 5 with center hole*

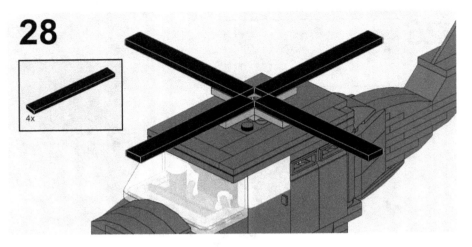

Figure 7-42. *Time to put on the 1 × 8 tiles on top to start the top rotor*

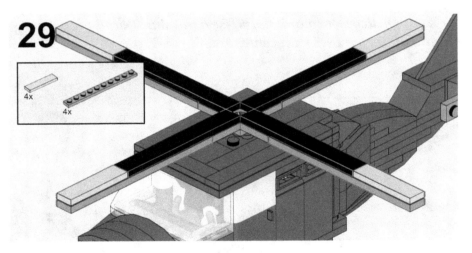

Figure 7-43. *Use the four 1 × 10 plates as shown, and then cap it off with the four 1 × 4 tiles*

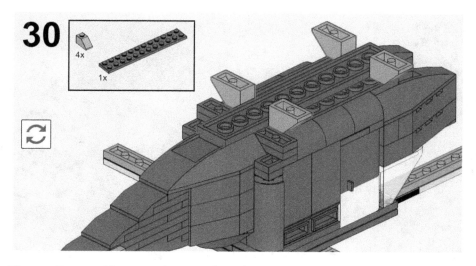

Figure 7-44. *After putting on the plate 2 × 12, put on the slope 45 2 × 1*

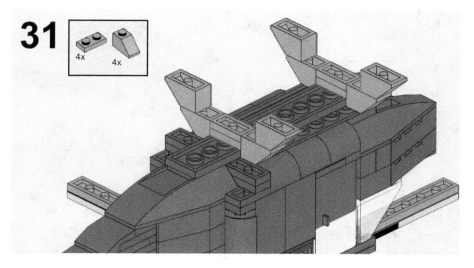

Figure 7-45. *Put on the four 1 × 2 plates, and then add the four slope 45 2 × 1 pieces*

32

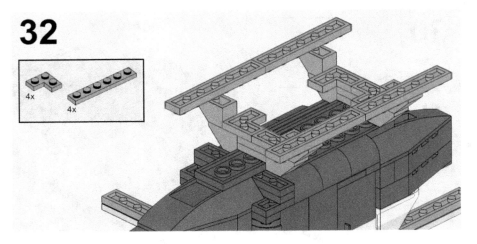

Figure 7-46. Add on the four plates 4 × 4 corner, and then add on the four 1 × 6 plates

33

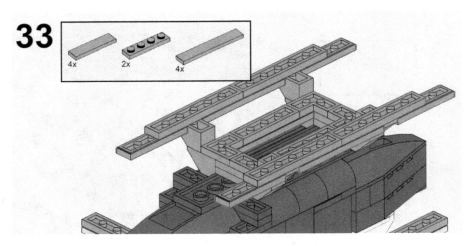

Figure 7-47. Use the 1 × 6 tiles to bridge areas, and the 1 × 4 plates hold them together in some places. The 1 × 4 tiles get used on the edge

Okay, so that is a basic helicopter, and if you want to improve the design, then by all means, give it a go! Chances are, you'll find better ways of building the top rotor and side rotor, and you might want to make one of those helicopters with two rotors on top! Again, I will leave it up to you.

Boats

Since I am not really devoting much here to water vehicles, I am not really going to devote a lot of time to boats, but I want to bring them up because this is a book about LEGO Worldbuilding, and you might want boats to be a part of your world.

If so, then maybe you're building your LEGO world, diorama, or whatever in some pool or something, because you might be doing something unconventional. There are some builders who use blue transparent bricks to make the illusion of water, and we'll get into that when we talk about detailing in the last chapter.

Like the first LEGO planes, early LEGO boats started out as quite blocky, and the first one didn't really float per se. In 1973, LEGO instructed some interesting shaped pieces to look like boats that were not blocky at all, as well as this interesting keel piece that acted as a weight to counter act the tipping. This started an entire fleet of LEGO boats that were very popular in the 1970s and 1980s, that I discussed in Chapter 1.

These are some parts of boats, some big, some small, if you really want to get your feet wet (or hands) working with them.

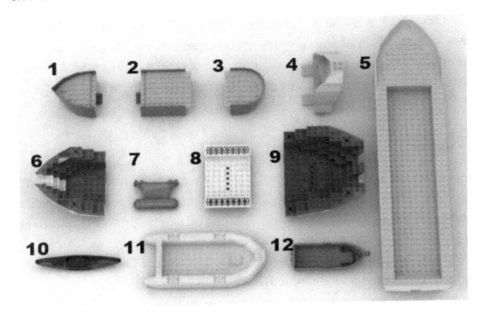

Figure 7-48. *Samples of LEGO boat parts*

1) Boat, hull smooth bow 5 × 6 × 3 1/3 (x145c01)

2) Boat, hull smooth middle 8 × 6 × 3 1/3 (x146c01)

3) Boat, hull smooth stern 6 × 6 × 3 1/3 (x147c01)

4) Boat, stern brick 7 × 16 × 7 with two windows (47992)

5) Boat, hull unitary 51 × 12 × 6 (54100c01)

6) Boat, hull small bow 12 × 12 × 5 1/3 (6050c02)

7) Boat, heel weighted 8 × 2 × 4 without bottom tab (x 149a)

8) Boat, hull small middle 8 × 12 (6054)

9) Boat, hull large stern 14 × 16 × 5 1/3 (2558c03)

10)   Boat, kayak (29110)

11)   Boat, rubber raft, large (62812)

12)   Boat, 14 × 5 × 2 with oarlocks (2551)

Of course, you can get certain boat pieces that will withstand the seas of a bathtub. The ones that are made of one piece are usually the ones that really float. Sadly, a lot of those really cool giant pirate ships will not. What is interesting is that the giant Titanic set also doesn't float, so go figure.

Conclusion

If you want to make some planes for your minifigs, then all you need to do is plan your plane (you saw what I did there). I recommend building around your minifigs, just so you can insure that they will all fit inside whatever cramped space is necessary for something that can travel through the air. You definitely need to plan for propulsion like a propeller or jet engines, doors that can open for loading and unloading, as well as landing gear.

When it comes to helicopters, most of the same rules apply. You really only need to have a place for the top rotor (or rotors) or a side rotor. Also, you want to put on some landing skids.

With boats, that can be pretty complex if you want them to float, but fortunately, LEGO provides pieces for that, if that floats your boat. Okay, that was really bad, so I think it's time we head toward the stars with spaceships!

CHAPTER 8

Setting Sights for the Stars: Building LEGO Spaceships

I'm sure everyone reading this book has seen *The Lego Movie*, and I'm sure everyone remembers the 1980s spaceman, voiced by Charlie Day of *It's Always Sunny in Philadelphia*. He's always got an excited look on his face as he is always ready to build a (feel free to yell this aloud) SPACESHIP!!!

I'm talking SPACESHIP in ALL CAPS with at least three exclamations points, and you might recall the scene in the LEGO movie where he just keeps trying to build a SPACESHIP!!! for his friends, only to discover that they don't need one at the time. When he is finally able to build the SPACESHIP!!! for the final battle, he gets really goes so over the top that he would have cracked that space helmet if he hadn't cracked it already. (As an aside, most LEGO Spacemen had that cracked bottom part of the helmet, and it is an excellent attention to detail that the animators went out of their way to put it in.)

Yeah, as a kid, much of my collection was Space LEGO, and for a good reason, too. They were the kits that had all of the really interesting pieces, and what really got my attention was the famed Galaxy Explorer. Now this was a set that was essentially a SPACESHIP!!!

© Mark Rollins 2024
M. Rollins, *Ultimate LEGO Worldbuilding and Architecture*, Maker Innovations Series,
https://doi.org/10.1007/979-8-8688-0521-9_8

Maybe you are Benny right now and have been antsy to no avail and you have been going through the first few chapters and really wanted to finally got your chance to figure out how to build your SPACESHIP!!! of choice. This chapter is going to teach you how to do all of that.

Spaceship Building 101

For example, you will need a strong foundation to build upon, because a spaceship has to be strong enough so you can lift it up without worrying if it will fall apart. You will also need to apply the principles of building a LEGO house, just so you can create rooms where your spacemen can dwell on their interstellar voyages. Your spacemen will also need to have realistic types of furniture, and I recommend always insuring that it is built into the walls and floors.

As far as the basic shape of the spaceship, that can be as simple or as complex as your imagination will allow. Personally, I don't recommend going too complex, as something like that can fall apart easily. I recommend spaceships that have a simple shape, something that you can sketch out very simply, like the Discovery from *2001: A Space Odyssey* or the fan-favorite, the Millennium Falcon. Yes, that Millenium Falcon has had several different LEGO versions over the years, and if you can get a hold of a set to help learn how to do spaceship modeling, I do recommend it. You can use the principles learned in the chapters on vehicles and aircraft in order to really get the shape of your spaceship right, such as the landing gear.

In short, this is where a lot of the lessons really start coming together, and like the creation of your base or any buildings, I highly recommend grabbing a napkin and pen are doing some crude sketches to create a plan, crude as it may be, of what to build.

For example, you could go for a spaceship that has plenty of wide-open spaces inside, so the astronauts won't feel so claustrophobic in their travels. Of course, this would mean that you would need to use a lot of pieces just to get all that, so you could go for cramped, something that real astronauts have to deal with daily.

I kind of went with something akin to the spaceships of *Star Trek* and *Star Wars*, with enough space to walk around in, but nothing huge like a gymnasium or auditorium. I also went with the idea that there is gravity on your spaceship, but if you want to create something like that, just be sure that there are a lot of places for the LEGO Spacemen to hold on to.

LEGO Base and Landing Gear

You will find that much of the building principles that I laid out in the past few chapters will be put into practice here in creating a spaceship (I'm going to stop with the all caps and exclamation points for simplicity's sake). Part of making certain that it will stay together is insuring that its base is thick and built with overlapping plates and bricks.

If you are going to build a strong base, then you will need to insure that you have some thrusters underneath to make certain that your ship can take off. I'm going assume that you will want to insure that your ship can do VTOL (Vertical Take-Off Landing). You can put on landing gear, and I recommend using hinge pieces so that landing gear can retract.

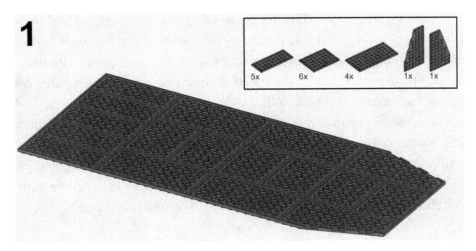

Figure 8-1. *Go ahead and line up all the 4 × 10, 6 × 8, and 6 × 12 plates with the wedge plate 12 × 6 left and right for a base, with studs facing down*

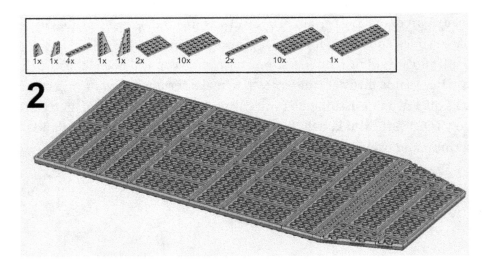

Figure 8-2. *Put on the 4 × 6, 4 × 10, 4 × 8, 4 × 12, 1 × 10, and 1 × 6 plates as shown, along with the wedge plate 6 × 3 and the wedge plate 3 × 2 left and right*

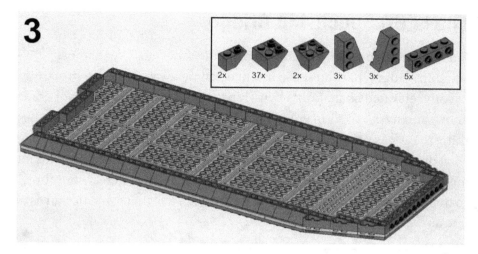

Figure 8-3. *Put on the wedge 3 × 2 left and right bricks, along with the bricks modified 1 × 4 with studs on the side. Put in the various slope inverted 45 2 × 2, 2 × 1, and the 2 × 2 double convex*

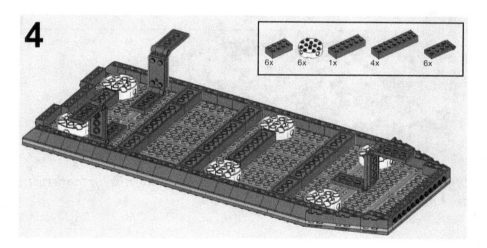

Figure 8-4. *Connect the two hinge plate 2 × 4 to make the landing gear. Put on the round brick 4 × 4, and then add all the 2 × 4, 2 × 6, and 2 × 8 bricks*

The LEGO Spaceship Bridge

I modeled my spaceship bridge after *Star Trek* because, yeah, most
starship bridges that you see in science fiction always have the captain
in some elevated chair. Is this how ships at sea have their bridges? I don't
know, and it isn't like I'm going for full realism here. I figured that the best
thing to do was probably just imitate that design.

I did go for the sliding door, because that's pretty much a standard for
any spaceship in any science fiction performance anywhere. I show how
to make one here if you are interested. In fact, I use that same design as an
entrance to the rooms.

Figure 8-5. *Use the pieces from this step to put together a workstation
as shown*

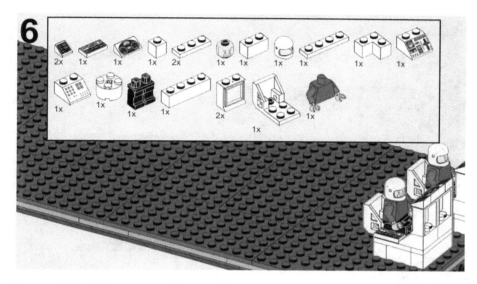

Figure 8-6. *Time to put in another workstation as shown, which is a mirror reflection of the last step*

Figure 8-7. *Time to assemble a captain's chair to sit in back of these two ensigns here. I'll let you decide if they need space helmets*

Figure 8-8. *Use the wedge 3 × 2 left and right, and use the brick 1 × 4 without bottom tubes for the front glass. Then use the round plate 1 × 1, with 1 × 2 tiles*

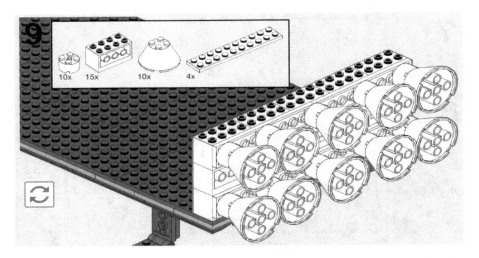

Figure 8-9. *Go ahead and used the modified brick 2 × 4, to make the back wall. Use the 2 × 10 plates to start the round brick 2 × 2 with the cone 4 × 4 × 2 to make thrusters*

246

Rooms

I decided to have a crew of just four, with a captain, two officers on the bridge, and an engineer type. I decided to give them each their own quarters, all equal sized, and I made two bathrooms. Yeah, I definitely decided to go with artificial gravity if I have toilets like these. I realize that going to the bathroom in space involves a lot of tubes that I didn't really want to replicate in LEGO. Note how each room has a bed built into the wall and window with at least a small view.

Please note how the interior walls are built so they will link with the exterior ones, and I recommend doing that just to get some strength going on. You will note that I used some hinged pieces so you can open some doors on the side for entry.

Figure 8-10. *Use the 1 × 1, 1 × 4, and 1 × 8 bricks to form the first level of the rooms*

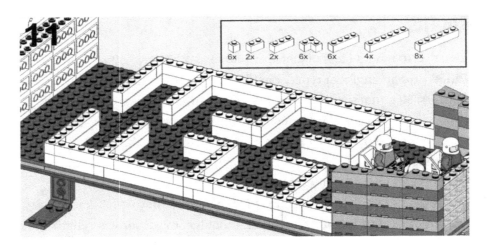

Figure 8-11. *Time to put on the 1 × 1, 2 × 1, 1 × 3, 1 × 4, and 2 × 2 corner and the 1 ×6 bricks for the second level of the rooms*

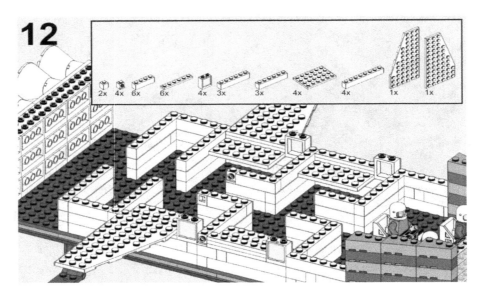

Figure 8-12. *Use the 1 × 1, 1 × 4, 1 × 6, and 1 × 8 bricks, along with the brick modified 1 × 1 with headlight. Put on the wedge plate 12 × 6 left and right with the 1 × 6 and 4 × 6 plates for the third level*

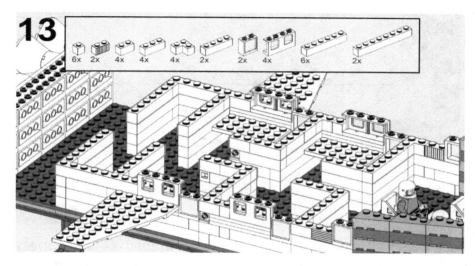

Figure 8-13. *Use the 1 × 1, 1 × 2 modified, 1 × 2, 1 × 3, 1 × 4, 1 × 6, and 1 × 8 with 2 × 2 corner bricks. Use the 1 × 4 × 2 plane and 1 × 2 × 2 flat window to fill the gaps*

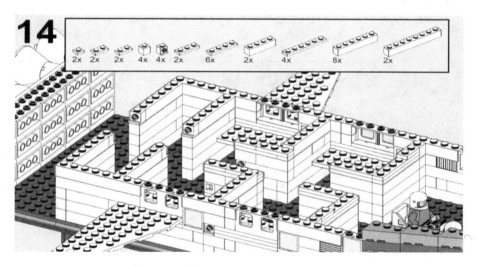

Figure 8-14. *Use the 1 × 1, 1 × 2, 1 × 3, 1 × 4, and 1 × 6 plates. Also put in the 1 × 1, 1 × 4, 1 × 6, 1 × 8, and 1 × 1 modified with headlight brick*

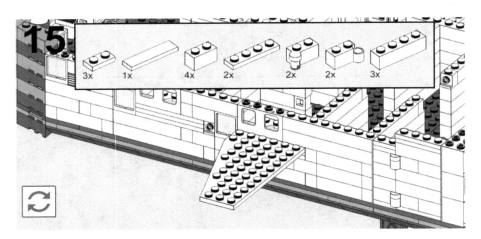

Figure 8-15. *Time to put in the side door with the 1 × 4 hinge bricks and 1 × 2 and 1 × 4 bricks. Put in the 1 × 2 and 1 × 4 plates and the 1 × 4 tile*

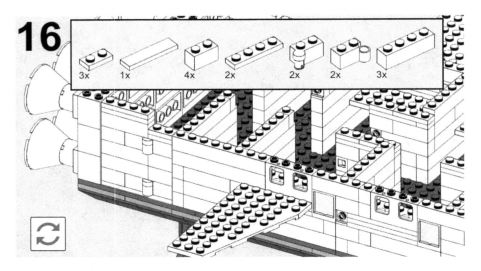

Figure 8-16. *Put in another side door with the 1 × 4 hinge bricks and 1 × 2 and 1 × 4 bricks. Put in the 1 × 2 and 1 × 4 plates and the 1 × 4 tile*

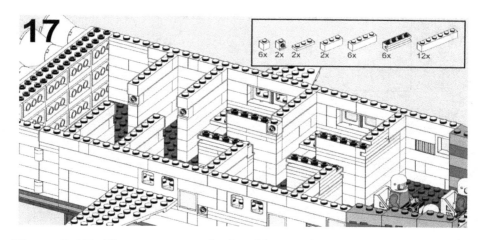

Figure 8-17. *Time to put on the final layer of the rooms which include the 1 × 1, 1 × 3, 1 × 4, and 1 × 6 and 1 × 1 modified headlight bricks. There is the 1 × 3 plate with the brick modified 1 × 4*

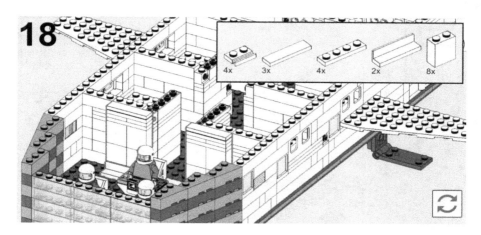

Figure 8-18. *Time to put in the double sliding doors that lead to the bridge, with 1 × 2 × 2 bricks, 1 × 4 plates, and 1 × 4 tiles. The 1 × 4 × 1 panel on the floor as well as the modified plate 1 × 2 with door rail*

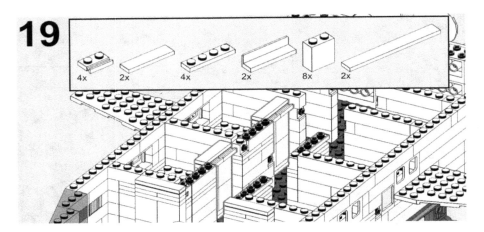

Figure 8-19. *Put the sliding doors on the bridge, with 1 × 2 × 2 bricks, 1 × 4 plates, and 1 × 4 tiles. The 1 × 4 × 1 panel on the floor as well as the modified plate 1 × 2 with door rail with the 1 × 8 tile*

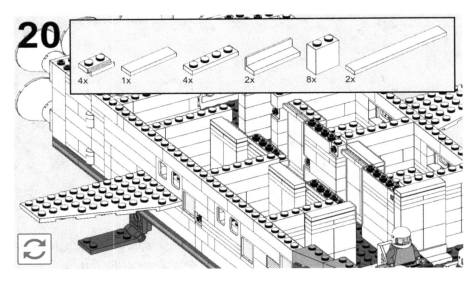

Figure 8-20. *Put the sliding doors on the bridge, with 1 × 2 × 2 bricks, 1 × 4 plates, and 1 × 4 tiles. The 1 × 4 × 1 panel on the floor as well as the modified plate 1 × 2 with door rail with the 1 × 8 tile*

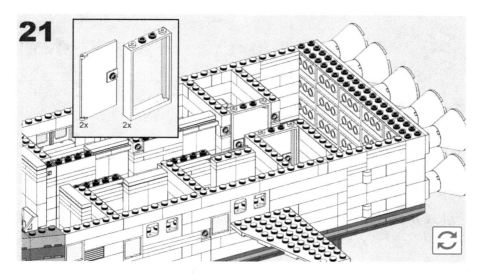

Figure 8-21. *This step uses door frame 1 × 4 × 6 and 1 × 4 × 6 doors for the bathrooms, and also add two toilets from Chapter 5*

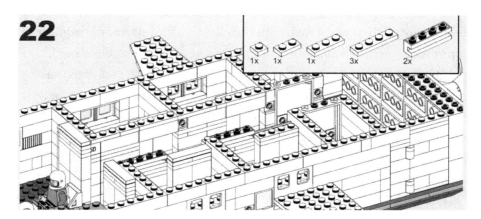

Figure 8-22. *Time to put in the 1 × 4 modified with channel and the 1 × 1, 1 × 2, 1 × 3, and 1 × 4 plates*

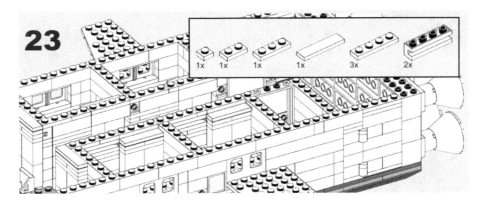

Figure 8-23. *Time to put in the 1 × 4 modified with channel and the 1 × 1, 1 × 2, 1 × 3, and 1 × 4 plates*

The Back and the Top

Okay, I have to admit, I don't know much about how space shuttles work, but I do know they usually have some kind of thrusters in the back, and I decided to go all out for maximum thrust. I don't know about installing a hyperdrive or warp drive, but that's getting into pseudoscience here.

Of course, since I'm going to have an enclosed area, I want to make certain that I have a way to open up the top so I can put the spacemen in there. I went for using hinge pieces that I have used before, atop places with tiles so it can easily flip up when needed. You will notice that I used some plates to really cap off the walls, and it gives the structure a lot of stability. You will also notice how I used windshield pieces for the bridge.

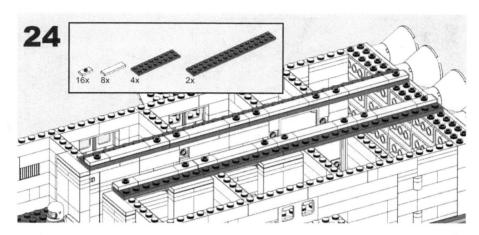

Figure 8-24. *Put on the 2 × 8 and 2 × 16 to start, and then put on the 1 × 4 tiles and the 1 × 2 modified tiles with stud in groove*

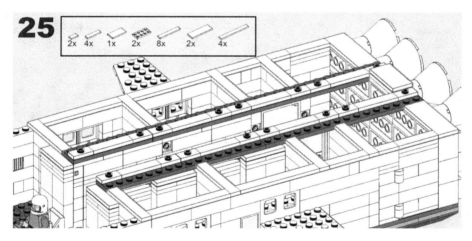

Figure 8-25. *Put on the 2 × 4 plates and then all the tiles like the 1 × 2, 1 × 4, 1 × 6, and 1 × 8, with the 2 × 4 and 2 × 6*

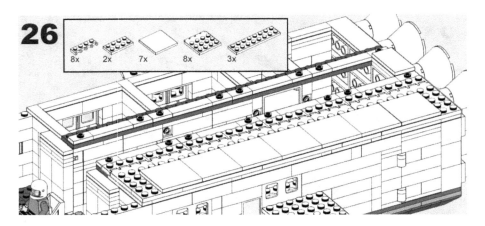

Figure 8-26. *Time to put on the top with the hinge plate 1 × 4 and the hinge vehicle roof 4 × 4. Use the 4 × 4 tiles to put on the 2 × 4 and 2 × 8 plates*

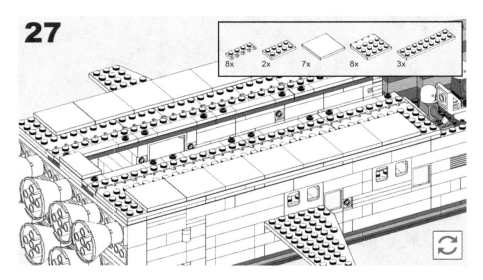

Figure 8-27. *Time to put on the top with the hinge plate 1 × 4 and the hinge vehicle roof 4 × 4. Use the 4 × 4 tiles to put on the 2 × 4 and 2 × 8 plates*

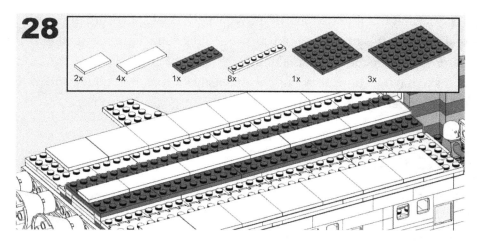

Figure 8-28. *With this step, you make a top. Put on the 1 × 8 plates underneath the 2 × 6, 6 × 6, and 6 × 8 plates, with the 2 × 6 and 2 × 4 tiles*

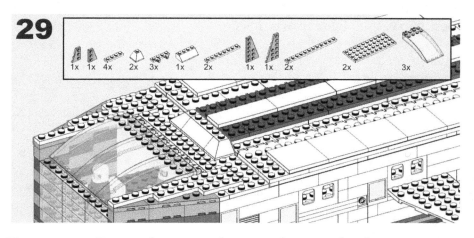

Figure 8-29. *Put on the 4 × 10 plates, and put on the slopes 45 2 × 4 and 2 × 2 double convex corner. Put on the wedge plate 6 × 3 and plate 3 × 2 left and right, as well as the 1 × 3, 1 × 6, and 1 × 10 plates. Put on the hinge plate 1 × 4 locking dual 1 finger and the windscreen 8 × 4 × 2 curved locking dual 2 fingers*

257

So, what is it that we have here? Well, we have a spaceship that can't really fly, but it is made for holding some LEGO Spacemen to head into outer space. I recommend making them "airtight" as best as you can, and it helps to have sections that can pop off easily for that, not to mention parts that can open up with a hinge.

Conclusion

When it comes to making a spaceship, it really is just a matter of creating a house that can fly. Well, it might not be able to fly, but think of it as making a house that can go into space. Of course, it has to be airtight, or at least as airtight as possible.

This is really where the imagination can run wild and capture all of those dreams of flight and heading to the stars. It is important that your spaceship has some kind of realistic functionality, so always give a way to open it up so minifigures can be inside.

CHAPTER 9

Going Giant with LEGO Robots and Animals

It's pretty clear that if you are trying to get to creating something real in LEGO, you should have stopped at the chapter just before spaceships. After all, when we get into spaceship territory that we get into *Star Wars/Star Trek* territory, I am going to continue to get even more into that with the creation of robots. I also want to get into more of the fantasy element, as this deals with animals, both real and fantastical.

Animals

If you just want to create animals, some already come created and made for minifig scale. That makes a lot of sense, because as I have said before, minifigs are actually pretty small, and most animals are also somewhat small.

Not only does LEGO make small animals, but they make big ones as well. I'm talking about dinosaurs and dragons, and some of them are just big hunks, but it is possible to just make them piece by piece.

© Mark Rollins 2024

M. Rollins, *Ultimate LEGO Worldbuilding and Architecture*, Maker Innovations Series, https://doi.org/10.1007/979-8-8688-0521-9_9

I decided to go ahead and make a dragon because I thought it would be a good example of how to do some kind of animal that is not only large but is essentially built from individual pieces to create something that looks like it would fit in a minifig world.

Now, before I get into that, I have to make a disclaimer. Some of these pieces are LEGO Technic, something that I said earlier that I wasn't going to discuss in this book. The fact is that they are pieces that allow a lot of flexibility, which is what you are going to need if you are making an animal or any other creation which has moving parts.

In fact, much of this dragon creation involves creating the individual parts and then snapping them all together. I'll start with this one at a time.

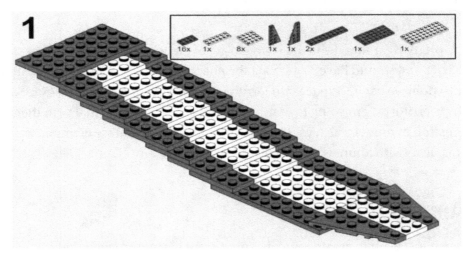

Figure 9-1. *Put on the wedge 6 × 3 plate (left and right), and then put on the 4 × 10, 2 × 6, and 2 × 8 plates. From there, put on the 4 × 4 and 2 × 4 plates in a stairstep formation with the 4 × 8 plate on top*

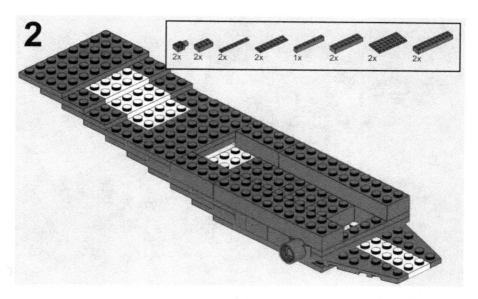

Figure 9-2. *Put on the technic 2 × 2 with peg hole and rotation joint socket, and then put on the 1 × 8, 2 × 8, and 4 × 8 plates and the 1 × 8, 2 × 4, 2 × 8, and 2 × 10 bricks as shown*

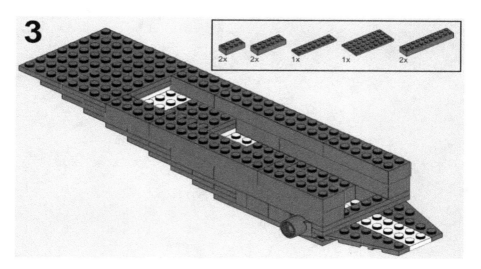

Figure 9-3. *Put on the 2 × 4, 2 × 6, and 2 × 10 bricks, as well as the 2 × 8 and 4 × 8 plates*

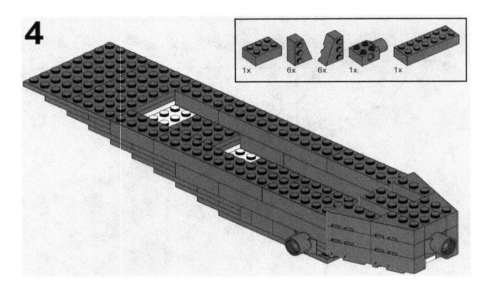

Figure 9-4. *Put on the wedge 3 × 2 left and right, as well as the 2 × 3 and 2 × 6 Bricks. Put on the technic modified brick 2 × 2 with rotation joint socket*

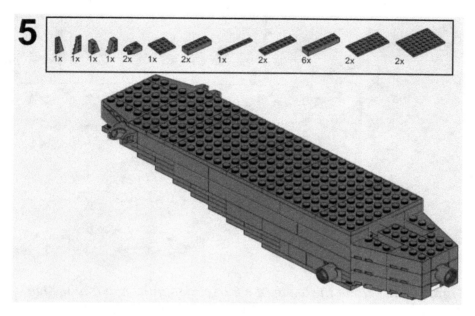

Figure 9-5. *Put on the technic brick modified with ball socket and then the wedge plates with wedge bricks, along with the plates and bricks*

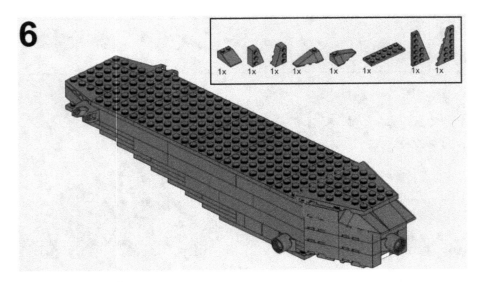

Figure 9-6. *Put on the wedge 4 × 2 triple left and right and wedge 2 × 3 left and right, along with the wedge plate 6 × 3 left and right. Put on the 2 × 6 plate and slope 33 3 × 2*

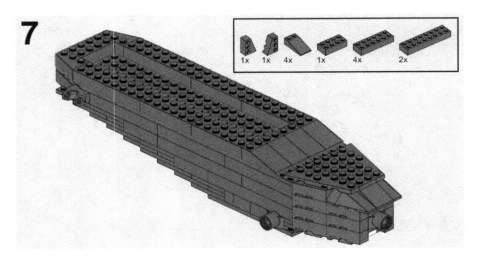

Figure 9-7. *Put on the 2 × 3 wedges, left and right, the 2 × 4 slope, and the 2 × 4, 2 × 6, and 2 × 8 bricks*

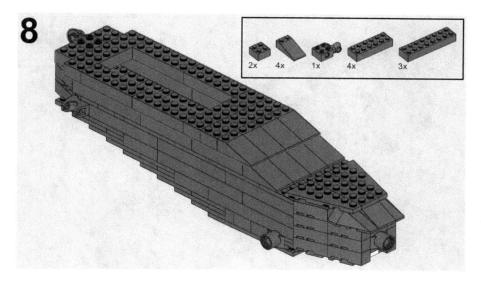

Figure 9-8. *Put on the 2 × 4 slopes, the technic brick modified 2 × 2 peg hole and rotation joint ball, and then the 2 × 2, 2 × 6, and 2 × 8 bricks*

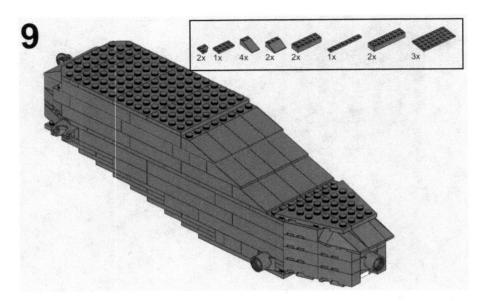

Figure 9-9. *Put in the wedge plate 2 × 2, the 2 × 4 slopes, the 2 × 3 slopes, and the 1 × 6, 2 × 4, and 4 × 8 plates, not to mention the 2 × 6 and 2 × 8 bricks*

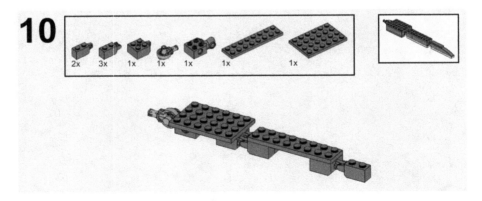

Figure 9-10. *Time to move on to the dragon tail. Put on the technic brick modified 2 × 2 peg hole and rotation joint ball, the hinge pieces, and the 2 × 8 and 4 × 6 plates*

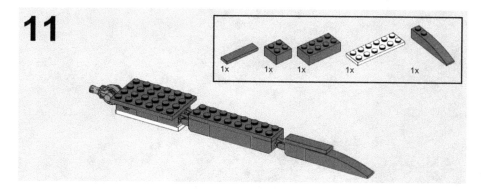

Figure 9-11. *Put on the 2 × 2 and 2 × 4 blocks and the 1 × 6 round brick. Then put on the 2 × 6 plate and 1 × 4 tile*

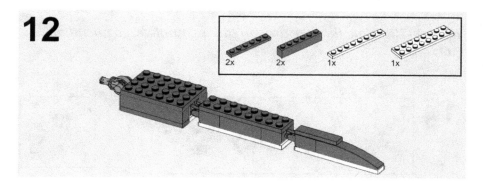

Figure 9-12. *Put on the 2 × 6 plates and bricks and then the 1 × 8 and 2 × 8 plates*

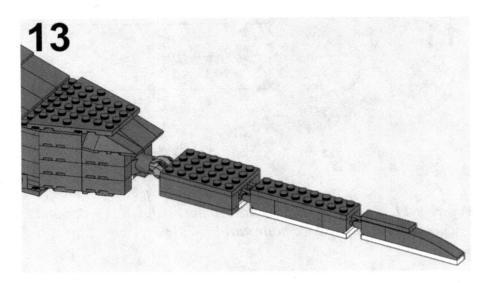

Figure 9-13. *Now that the dragon tail is complete, go ahead and put it on*

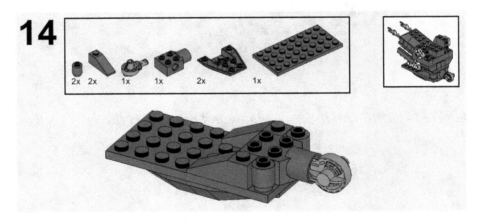

Figure 9-14. *Put on the technic hinge pieces, the 1 × 1 round pieces, the 1 × 3 slopes, and the 4 × 8 plates*

Figure 9-15. *Put on the 2 × 3 plate, the 2 × 1 bracket, and the 1 × 1 tooth plates*

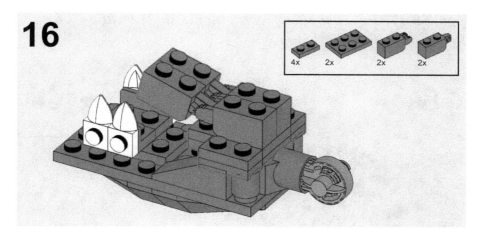

Figure 9-16. *Put on the two 2 × 3 and 1 × 2 plates and the hinge pieces*

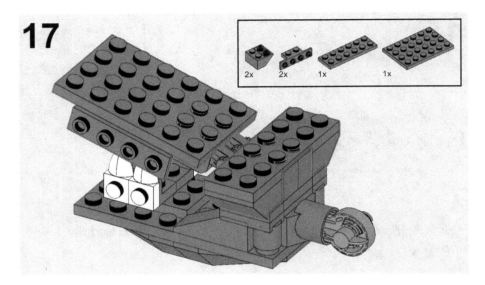

Figure 9-17. *Put on the 2 × 2 reverse slopes, the 2 × 6 and 4 × 8 plates, and then the 2 × 4 bracket*

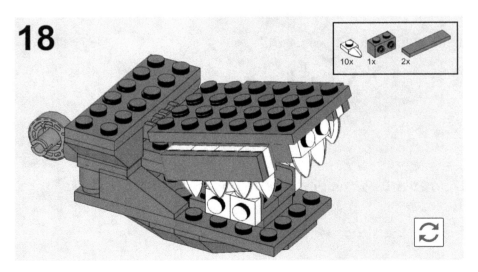

Figure 9-18. *Put on the 1 × 2 brick studs on the side, the 1 × 1 plates with tooth, and the 1 × 4 tiles*

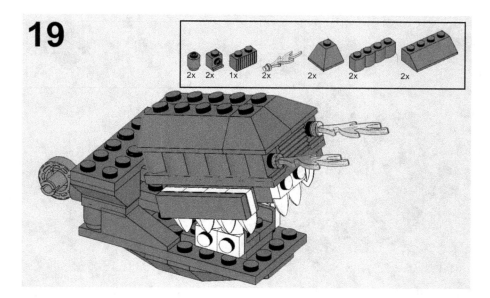

Figure 9-19. *Put on the 1 × 1 round brick, the 1 × 2 modified brick, the 1 × 4 curvy bricks, and the 2 × 4 slope and the 2 × 2 triple slopes with the flame elements*

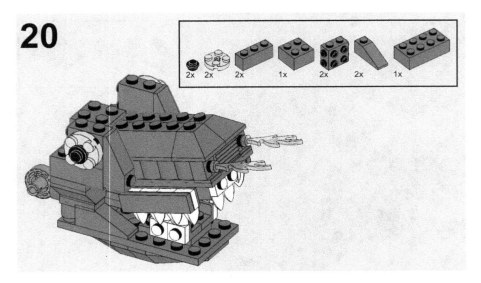

Figure 9-20. *Put on the 1 × 2 × 2 with studs on the side and then the 1 × 3, 2 × 2, and 2 × 4 bricks. Use the 2 × 2 round plate and the 1 × 1 round plate for the eyes, and put on the 1 × 3 slopes*

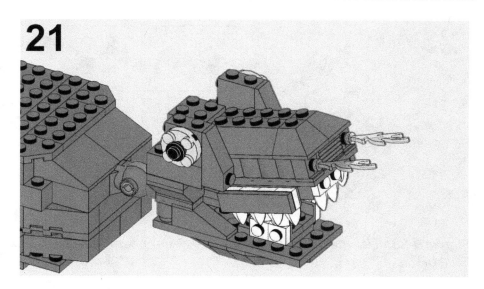

Figure 9-21. *Attach the dragon head to the dragon body*

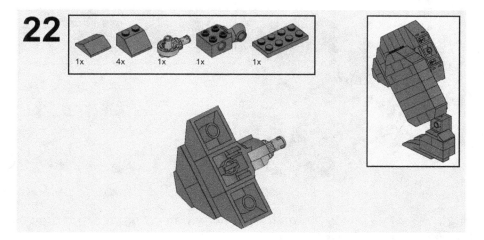

Figure 9-22. *Time to start the dragon legs. Use the technic hinges, as well as the 2 × 2 45 slopes, and the 2 × 2 slope, and the 2 × 4 plate*

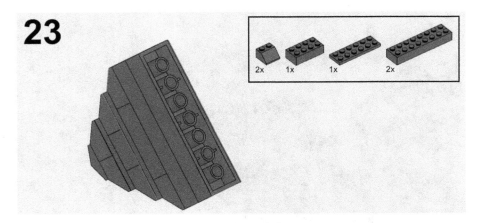

Figure 9-23. *Use the 2 × 6 plate, the 2 × 2 45 slopes, and the 2 × 4 and 2 × 8 bricks*

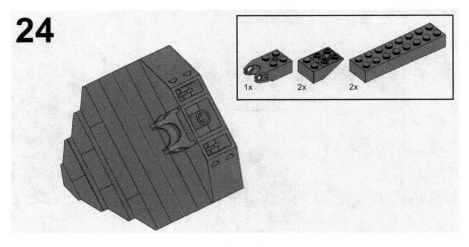

Figure 9-24. *Time to put on a technic ball socket holder, and then put on the inverted slopes 2 × 3 and the 2 × 8 bricks*

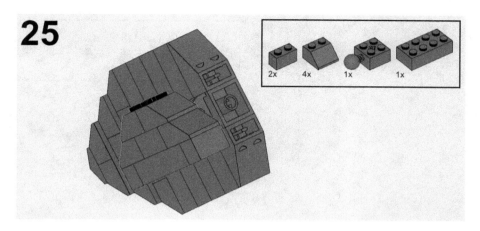

Figure 9-25. *Use the technic 2 × 2 with ball, the 2 × 2 45 slope, and the 2 × 4 brick and 1 × 2 bricks*

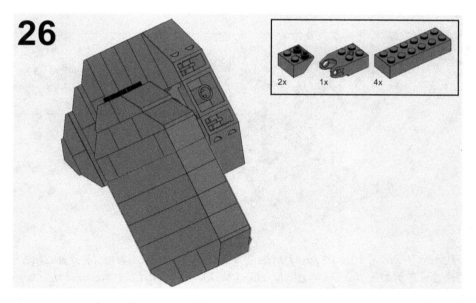

Figure 9-26. *Use the inverted 2 × 2 45 slope, the 2 × 2 socket holder, and the 2 × 6 bricks*

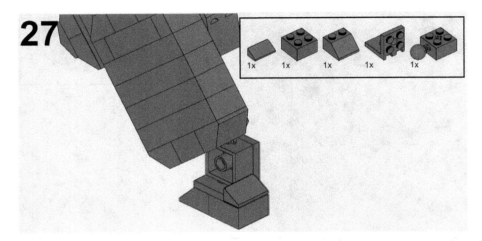

Figure 9-27. *Time use the 1 × 2 and 2 × 2 slope, the 2 × 2 with ball, and the 2 × 2 angle bracket with the 2 × 2 brick*

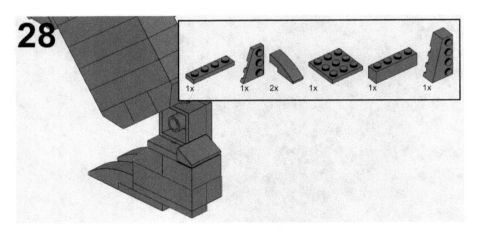

Figure 9-28. *Time to put in the 2 × 3 wedge plates, the 2 × 4 wedge, the 3 × 3 plate, the 1 × 4 plate, the 1 × 4 brick, and the curved brick*

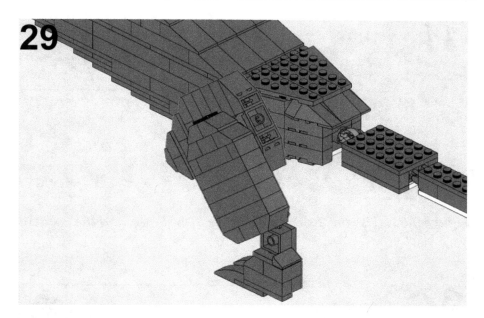

Figure 9-29. *Time to put on the dragon's back left leg*

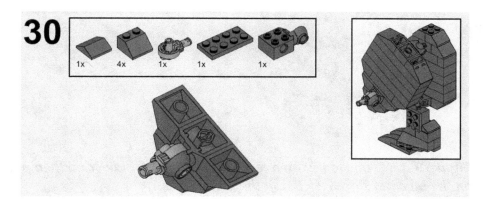

Figure 9-30. *Time to work on the dragon right back leg. Use the technic hinges as well as the 2 × 2 45 slopes, and the 2 × 2 slope, and the 2 × 4 plate*

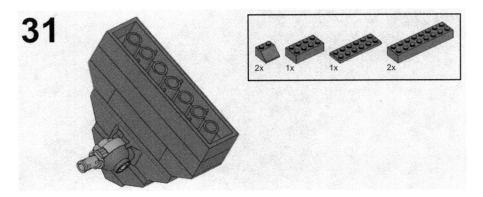

Figure 9-31. *Use the 2 × 6 plate, the 2 × 2 45 slopes, and the 2 × 4 and 2 × 8 bricks*

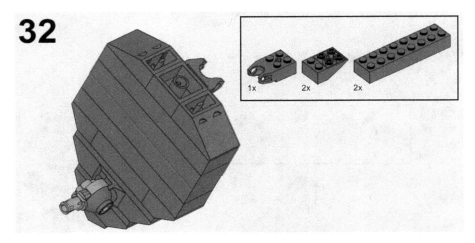

Figure 9-32. *Time to put on a technic ball socket holder, and then put on the inverted slopes 2 × 3 and the 2 × 8 bricks*

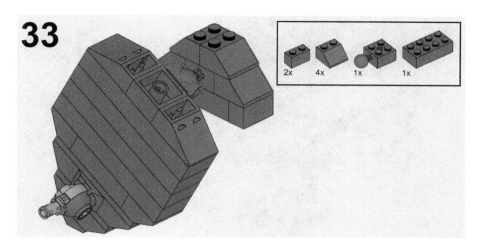

Figure 9-33. *Use the technic 2 × 2 with ball, the 2 × 2 45 slope, the 2 × 4 brick, and 1 × 2 bricks*

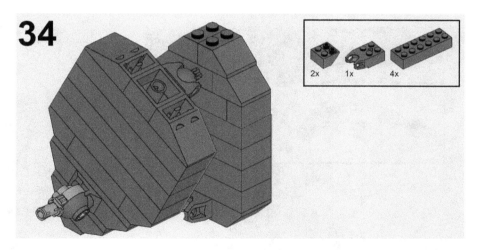

Figure 9-34. *Use the inverted 2 × 2 45 slope, the 2 × 2 socket holder, and the 2 × 6 bricks*

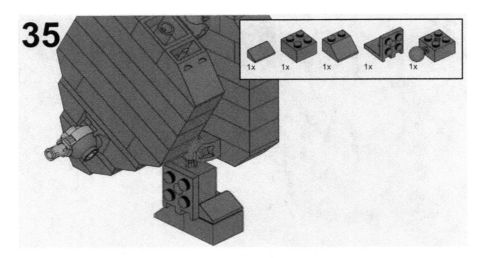

Figure 9-35. *Time to use the 1 × 2 and 2 × 2 slope, the 2 × 2 with ball, and the 2 × 2 angle bracket with the 2 × 2 brick*

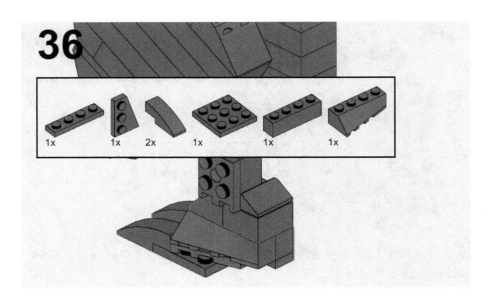

Figure 9-36. *Time to put in the 2 × 3 wedge plates, the 2 × 4 wedge, the 3 × 3 plate, the 1 × 4 plate, the 1 × 4 brick, and the curved brick*

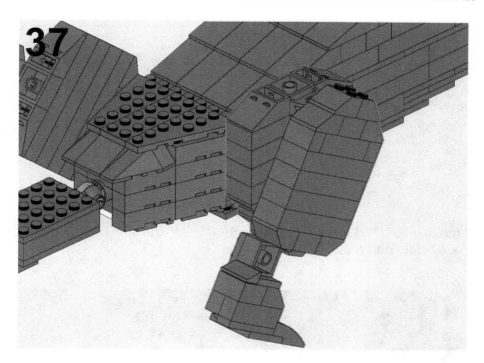

Figure 9-37. *Go ahead and attach the right back leg on the dragon*

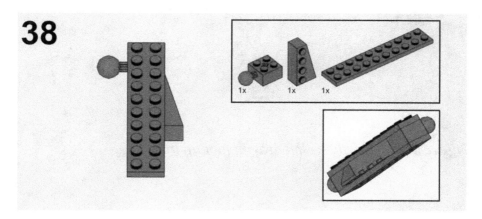

Figure 9-38. *Time to work on the left front foot with a 2 × 10 plate, a 1 × 4 brick wedge right, and a technic 2 × 2 with ball*

281

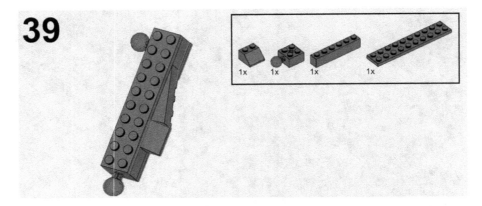

Figure 9-39. Put on the 2 × 2 45 slope, the technic 2 × 2 with ball, 1 × 6 brick, and the 2 × 10 plate

Figure 9-40. Put on the left dragon foot up front

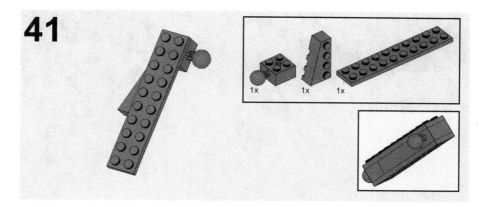

Figure 9-41. *Time to work on the right front foot with a 2 × 10 plate, a 1 × 4 brick wedge left, and a technic 2 × 2 with ball*

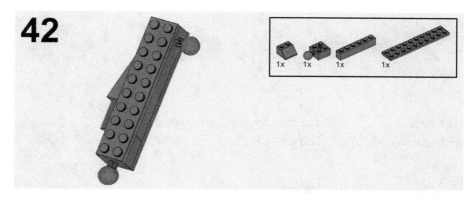

Figure 9-42. *Put on the 2 × 2 45 slope, the technic 2 × 2 with ball, 1 × 6 brick, and the 2 × 10 plate*

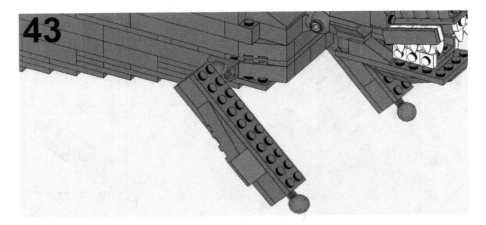

Figure 9-43. *Put on the right front foot on the dragon*

Figure 9-44. *Time to start a dragon's paw. Put on the 45 2 × 2 slope on the 2 × 3 tile, and then put on the 2 × 2 socket*

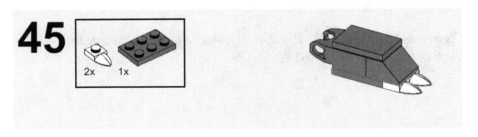

Figure 9-45. *Time to put on the 2 × 3 plate with the 1 × 1 plates with tooth*

Figure 9-46. *Go ahead and make another dragon's paw, and then put them both on the front*

Robots

Similar to animals, LEGO has minifigs that are, for lack of a better word, robots. I mean, you can make other mechanical beings that are minifig sized, and you can also make some that are minifig sized yourself.

It is also possible to make some kind of robot that is part human, part machine. I'm not talking about Robocop, but think of this as an exoskeleton. This can come small and large.

The one that I am making is a giant robot, and it is made so the midsection can open up, and you can put a minifig in there. It has arms with several points of articulation, but not so on the legs.

For the legs, I used a very old LEGO technique with turntable pieces that allow a simple step by step walking that is really just shifting feet. I could have used other joint pieces to make feet, and they would have been better if you want to pose the robot, but in LEGO, you often have to accept the stillness of your creation.

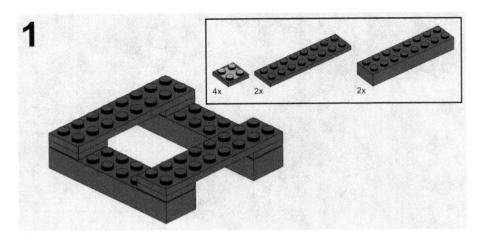

Figure 9-47. *Go on and put down the 2 × 8 bricks, with the turntables, and then put the 2 × 8 plate on them*

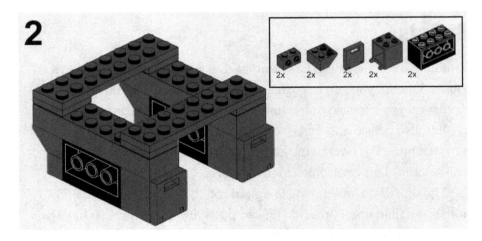

Figure 9-48. *Put on a 2 × 4 × 2 modified bricks with holes on the sides, slope inverted 45 2 × 2, modified brick 1 × 2 with studs on one side, and 2 × 2 × 2 container*

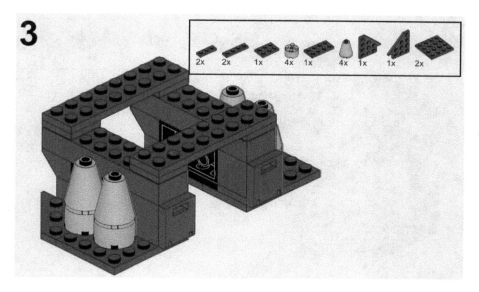

Figure 9-49. *Use the wedge plate 4 × 4 wing left and right, with the 1 × 3, 1 × 4, 2 × 3, 2 × 4, and 4 × 4 Plates. Put on the brick round 2 × 2 and the cone 2 × 2 × 2*

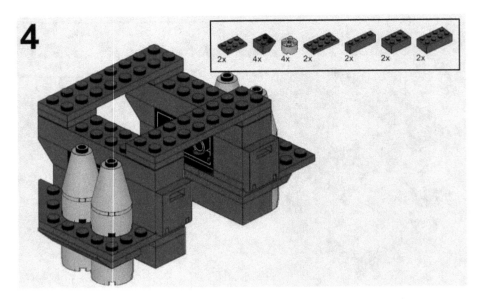

Figure 9-50. *Put on the 2 × 3 and 2 × 4 plates. Put on the inverted slope 45 2 × 2 and the 1 × 4, 2 × 3, and 2 × 4 bricks. Then put on the 2 × 2 round bricks*

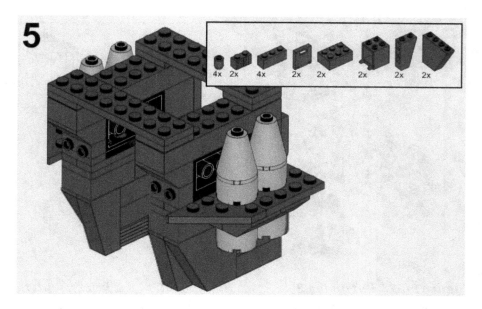

Figure 9-51. *Put on the inverted slope 75 2 × 1 × 3 and the inverted slope 60 4 × 1 × 3. Add on the 1 × 1 round, the 1 × 2 brick modified, the 1 × 3 and 2 × 3 bricks, and the 2 × 2 × 2 containers*

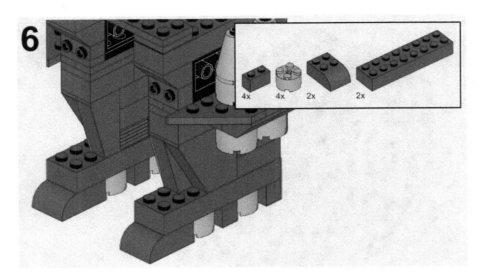

Figure 9-52. *Put on the 2 × 8 brick and then the 1 × 2 bricks, with the 2 × 2 round and the slope curved 3 × 2 with 4 studs*

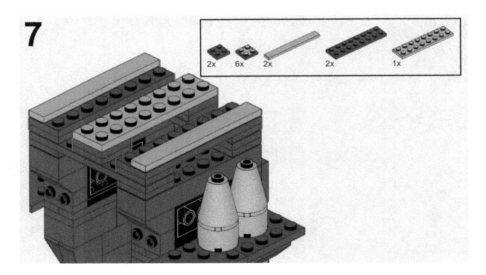

Figure 9-53. *Put on the 2 × 2 turntables and the 2 × 2 and 2 ×8 plates Put on the 1 × 8 tiles*

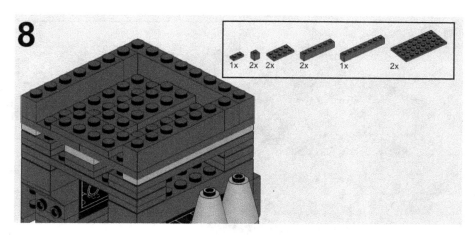

Figure 9-54. *Put on the 4 × 8, 1 × 2, and 2 × 4 plates. Then put on the 1 × 1, 1 × 6, and 1 × 8 bricks*

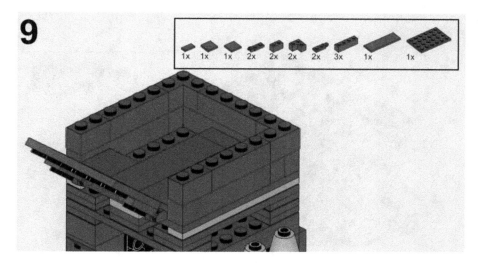

Figure 9-55. *Put on the hinges with the 4 × 6 plate. Put on the 1 × 2, 2 × 2, and 2 × 6 tiles. Put on the 1 × 2 and 2 × 2 corner and 1 × 4 plates*

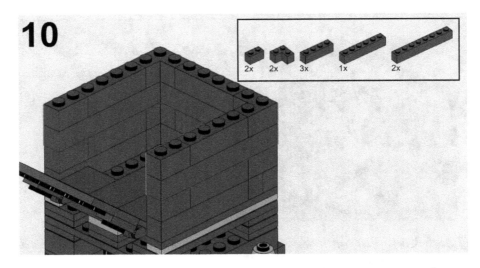

Figure 9-56. *Put up more levels with 1 × 2 and 2 × 2 corner and 1 × 4, 1 × 6, and 1 × 8 bricks*

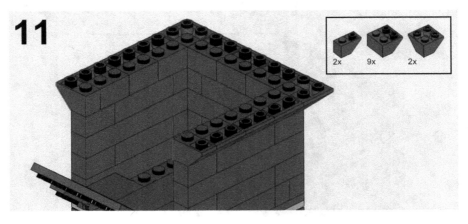

Figure 9-57. *Use the inverted slope 2 × 2, 1 × 2, and the 2 × 2 double convex*

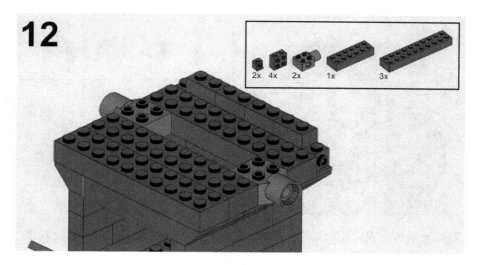

Figure 9-58. *Put on the technic brick modified 2 × 2 with rotation joint socket, the brick modified 1 × 2 × 1 2/3 with studs on the side, and the 1 × 1 modified brick with headlight. Put on the 2 × 6 and 2 × 8 bricks*

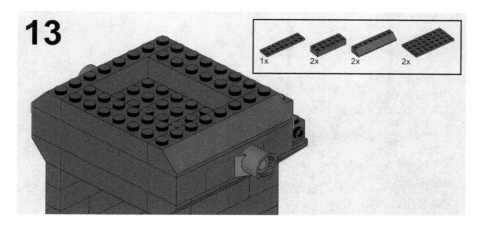

Figure 9-59. *Put on the 2 × 8 and 4 × 8 plates. Put on the 2 × 6 bricks and the 1 × 8 slope 45*

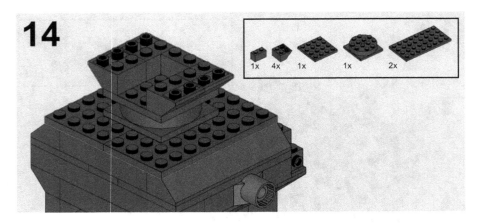

Figure 9-60. *Put on the 4 × 8 plates, the turntable 4 × 4 square base, the 2 × 2 45 inverted slopes, and the 1 × 2 brick*

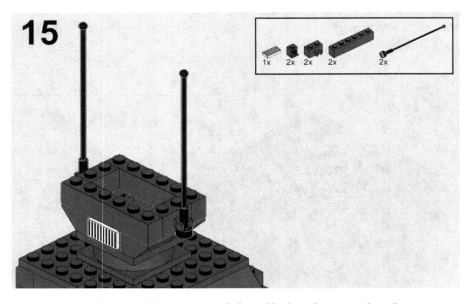

Figure 9-61. *Put on the 1 × 1 with headlight, the 1 × 6 brick, the modified brick 1 × 2 split U clip thick, the 1 × 2 tiles, and the antenna whip 8H*

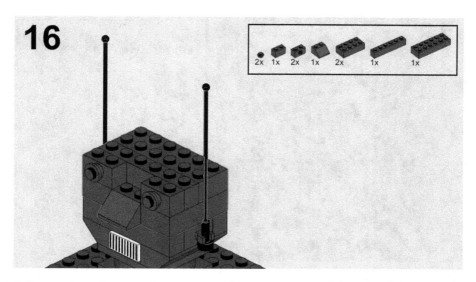

Figure 9-62. *Put on the 45 2 × 2 slope, 1 × 2 modified with stud on the side, the 2 x 2 round, and the 1 × 2, 2 × 4, 1 × 6, and 2 × 6 bricks*

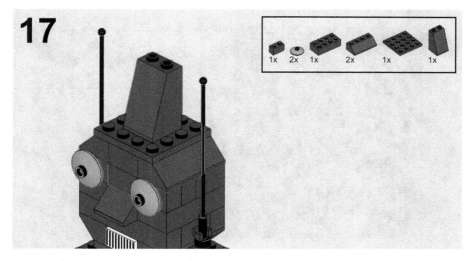

Figure 9-63. *Put on the 2 × 4 slope 45, the dish 2 × 2 inverted, 4 × 4 plate, slope 75 2 × 2 × 3, and the dish 2 × 2 inverted*

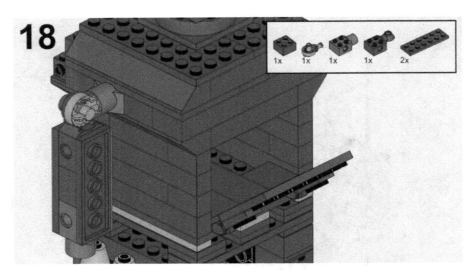

Figure 9-64. *Put on the technic rotation joint ball loop, the 2 × 2 with rotation joint ball half, and the technic 2 × 2 peg hold and rotation joint. Use the 2 × 2 brick and the 2 × 6 plate*

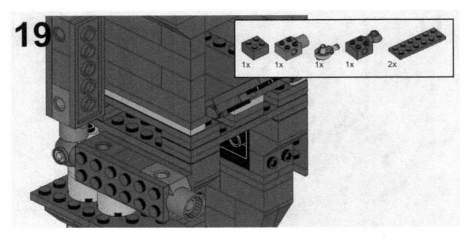

Figure 9-65. *Put on the technic rotation joint ball loop, the 2 × 2 with rotation joint ball half, and the technic 2 × 2 peg hold and rotation joint. Use the 2 × 2 brick and the 2 × 6 plate*

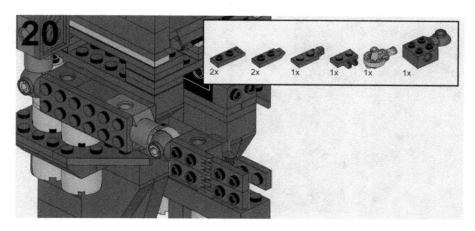

Figure 9-66. *Put on the technic rotation joint ball loop and the 2 × 2 with rotation joint ball half. Use the 1 × 2 hinge pieces and the 1 × 2 hinge*

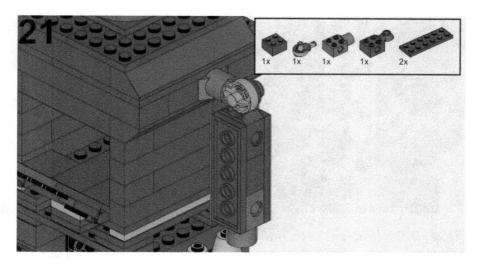

Figure 9-67. *Put on the technic rotation joint ball loop, the 2 × 2 with rotation joint ball half, and the technic 2 × 2 peg hold and rotation joint. Use the 2 × 2 brick and the 2 × 6 plate*

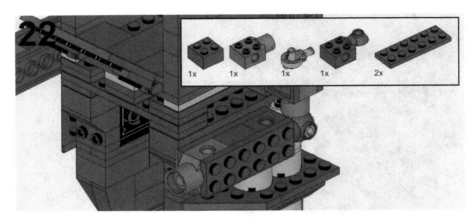

Figure 9-68. *Put on the technic rotation joint ball loop, the 2 × 2 with rotation joint ball half, and the technic 2 × 2 peg hold and rotation joint. Use the 2 × 2 brick and the 2 × 6 plate*

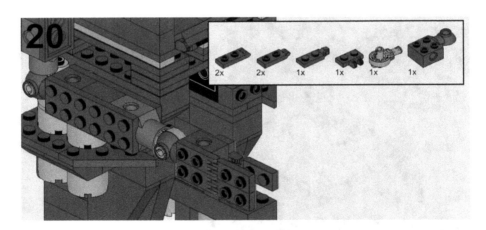

Figure 9-69. *Put on the technic rotation joint ball loop, the 2 × 2 with rotation joint ball half, and the technic 2 × 2 peg hold and rotation joint. Use the 2 × 2 brick and the 2 × 6 plate*

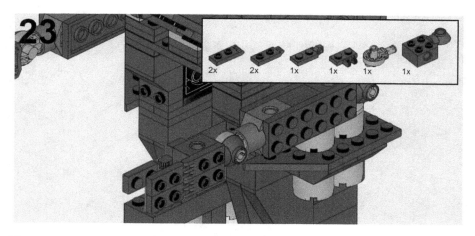

Figure 9-70. *Put on the technic rotation joint ball loop and the 2 × 2 with rotation joint ball half. Use the 1 × 2 hinge pieces and the 1 × 2 hinge*

Just to let you know, you don't need to make the robot in this manner with its legs that can slowly walk. You can make it so the robot has very active bendable limbs, like the dragon. In fact, this is the dragon if it is posed standing upright.

Figure 9-71. *What happens when the dragon is put up in a standing position*

I'm going to be the first to admit that I honestly don't prefer to do organic beasts with LEGO, but I'm wondering if this dragon and the robot can be made to look better with a bit of detailing.

Conclusion

Building a giant animal and building a massive robot in LEGO minifig scale requires very similar building practices. The real trick is figuring out beforehand what kind of articulation you are going to use at any bending areas, such as elbows, knees, and any other types of joints.

Once you get the basic form down, it really is about adding as much details as you can to make your LEGO creation as realistic as possible, and this is where detail comes in.

CHAPTER 10

Detailing a LEGO Creation and Final Thoughts

American architect Ludwig Mies van der Rohe once said "God is in the details," which means that details really matter, which will be the focus for this chapter. By the way, some say that Ludwig Mies van der Rohe also said "the devil is in the details." So which is it? Well, let's find out together.

You might notice that all of the models that I have are pretty minimal, as in, it is recognizable as the objects that they are, but they could use a little bit of upgrading. Most of that is done on purpose, because like I said before, this isn't a book that just tells you what to make, but give you an idea for creations that you can make.

Base

I will start with Chapters 2 and 3, because I instructed you how to make a great platform, but we all know that life is not just flat, as it is very diverse in its levels and lots of vegetation including trees, bushes, and grass.

© Mark Rollins 2024
M. Rollins, *Ultimate LEGO Worldbuilding and Architecture*, Maker Innovations Series,
https://doi.org/10.1007/979-8-8688-0521-9_10

When it comes to making trees, that's where you can get really creative as they can range from large to very large. You will need a lot of brown pieces, and you can also do a little bit of those vegetation pieces.

House and Furniture

For this, I have found that it is really good to look at a house and make it look like someone actually lives there. Fortunately, Stud.io allows its users to remove bricks and put in others for creating pictures, not to mention other details.

For example, if you add some 2 × 2 tiles to the kitchen area, you suddenly have what looks like an actual kitchen with alternating black and white.

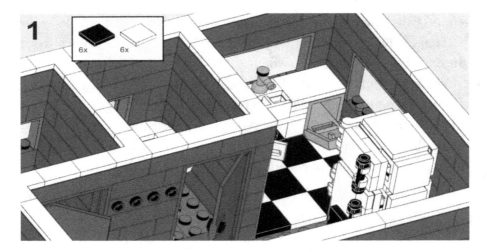

Figure 10-1. *Using the application of 2 × 2 black and white tiles, you can make a good representation of a kitchen floor*

It is also good to use 1 × 1 tiles that can be used in the bathroom, and I decided to use blue tiles that matched the walls. It definitely creates something great.

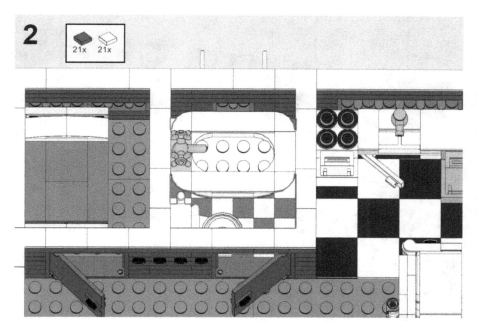

Figure 10-2. *Using 1 × 1 blue and white tiles, you will have a good representation of a bathroom floor*

Too bad I can't really do anything about the carpet. I guess LEGO doesn't have a proper texture for carpet, but it can be argued that the studs create a general ruddy surface, not unlike shag carpeting.

While we're on the subject of decoration, this would be a good time to talk about doing something about the blank walls. This is where you might have to do some redesign and add tile pieces that look like posters, such as the map ones.

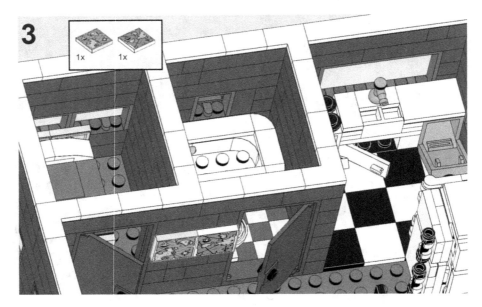

Figure 10-3. *With the application of some modified bricks and some specially decorated 2 × 2 tiles, you have yourself some posters*

Cars and Planes

All right, now that you have the car, you are going to need a road for it. I'm not going to go into great detail about how you can do a road, as I would rather just show it.

You can see that I used a lot of gray tile pieces, along with some yellow tiles for the lines in the middle. It took a lot of them just to make this, and there are a lot more cracks down in the road, more than in a real concrete road.

It's a small road that I put on the base that I created in Chapters 2 and 3, but it does work, and hey, I just put some duplicate versions of the Dodge Charger SXT in different colors.

Figure 10-4. *The addition of a road, along with some houses to the base*

You might also notice that I took the time to add in some houses, and yes, they are the houses from Chapter 4, but with different colors. I'm going to be going back to this base with its decor later, but I want to talk about other subjects first.

That comes for airplanes, who will definitely need some places to land, and there are all kinds. You are going to need to create something the size of a runway to do that, using the same principles for building a road. Also, if you are on a plane before it takes off, and you usually have to wait quite a long time, take note of all the vehicles and equipment and lighting around the runway and do your best to imitate it.

Spaceships

Now, this is where it gets really interesting. I think since the first *Star Wars* movie, we are used to seeing spaceships that have these incredibly rough textures. Part of that might have stemmed from old comics, where artists like Jack Kirby would make these gigantic tech things and put all kinds of detail on it so it looked like it could actually do something incredible.

In an interview with Paul Huston, a model maker for the original *Star Wars* movie of 1977, he discusses how to create a "mechanical look" from Syd Mead. If you aren't familiar with Syd Mead, he was a very influential designer of a lot of science fiction works such as *Blade Runner* and *Aliens*. The idea of creating a spaceship or some kind of futuristic vehicle is about creating a basic geometric shape and add details to make it look like things had some kind of function.

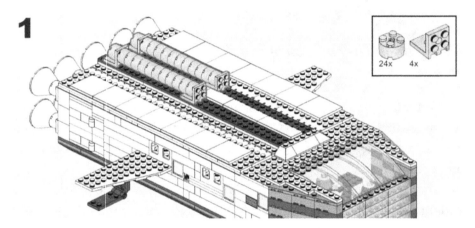

Figure 10-5. *Use the 2 × 2 brackets with the 2 × 2 round bricks*

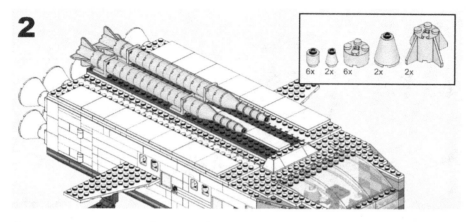

Figure 10-6. *Put on the rest of the 2 × 2 round bricks, with the 2 × 2 × 2 cones and 2 × 2 × 2 round bricks with fins. Add on the round 1 × 1 bricks and cone 1 × 1*

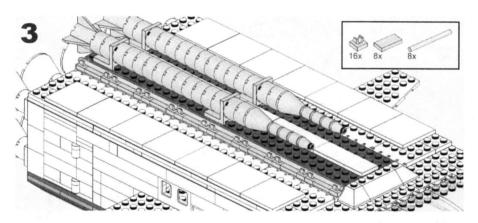

Figure 10-7. *Put on the tile modified 1 × 1 (with open O clip) with the 1 × 2 tiles, and then put on the 4 M bars*

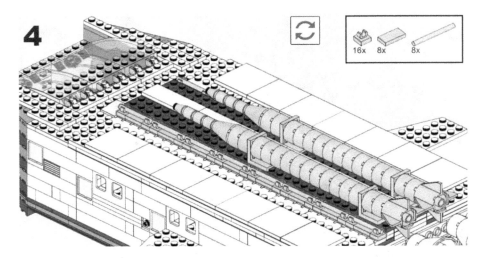

Figure 10-8. *Put on the tile modified 1 × 1 (with open O clip) with the 1 × 2 tiles, and then put on the 4 M bars*

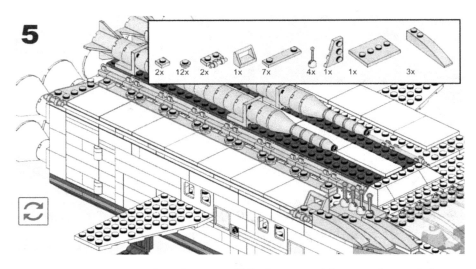

Figure 10-9. *Put on the plate modified 1 × 4 with 2 studs, and then put on the 1 × 1 plate and round plates. Put on the slope curved 6 × 1, tile modified 1 × 2, and plate modified 1 × 2(with bar handle). Then put on the tile modified 3 × 4 with studs in center and the antenna small base*

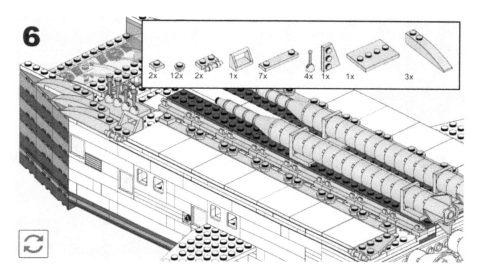

Figure 10-10. *Put on the plate modified 1 × 4 with 2 studs, and then put on the 1 × 1 plate and round plates. Put on the slope curved 6 × 1, tile modified 1 × 2, and plate modified 1 × 2(with bar handle). Then put on the tile modified 3 × 4 with studs in center and the antenna small base*

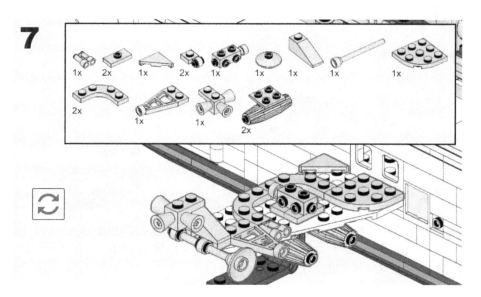

Figure 10-11. *Put on the engine strakes 2 × 2 on the bottom of the wing as shown, with the rest of the pieces on top*

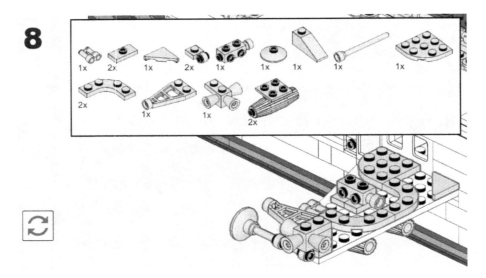

Figure 10-12. *Put on the engine strakes 2 × 2 on the bottom of the wing as shown, with the rest of the pieces on top*

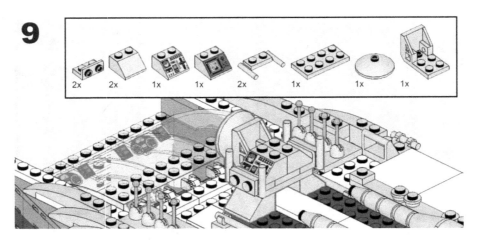

Figure 10-13. *Put on the slope 45 2 × 2 and then the 2 × 4 plate. Put on the bracket 3 × 2 (2 × 2 inverted) and the bracket 1 × 2 (1 × 2 inverted). Put on the rest as shown*

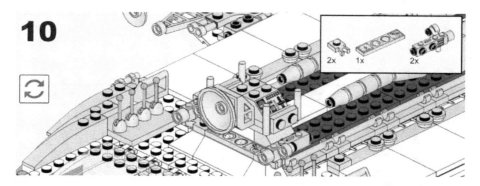

Figure 10-14. *Put on the plate modified 1 × 1 with U clip thick, and then add the 1 × 4 tile with minifigure utensil camera with side sight*

Robots and Animals

When it came to the dragon, I really felt that details really matter, particularly when it comes to making something that is essentially square and making it feel organic. What I have given in Chapter 9 is a basic form, with only minimal details like claws and teeth, what you would expect to even identify it as a dragon.

However, once more details are added, like spines and wings, it starts to become something great all on its own. Not only that, if it is posed in certain positions, it becomes super lifelike.

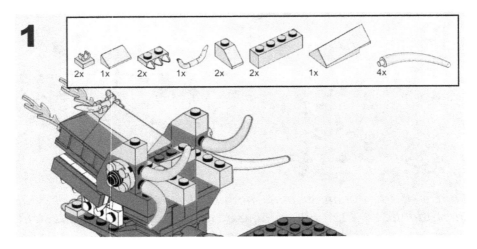

Figure 10-15. *Put on the horns, slopes, modified plates, modified tiles, and bricks to put more detail on the face*

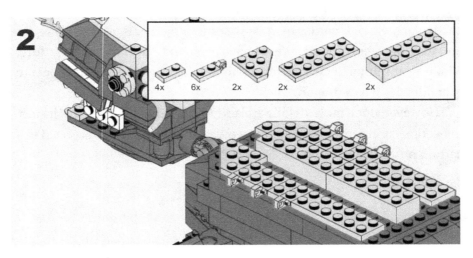

Figure 10-16. *Put on the wedge plate 3 × 3, along with the bricks, plates, and the 1 × 2 hinges*

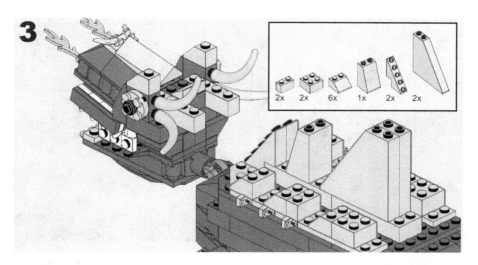

Figure 10-17. *Put on the slope 53 3 × 1 × 3 1/3 and the other slopes and bricks*

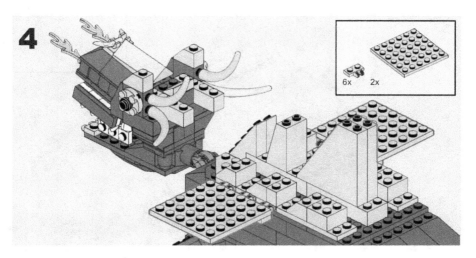

Figure 10-18. *Put on the hinge plate 1 × 2 and the 6 × 6 plates*

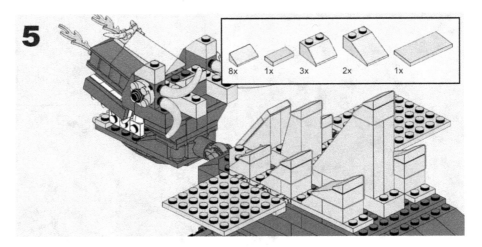

Figure 10-19. *Put on the slopes and tiles to complete the spikes on the back*

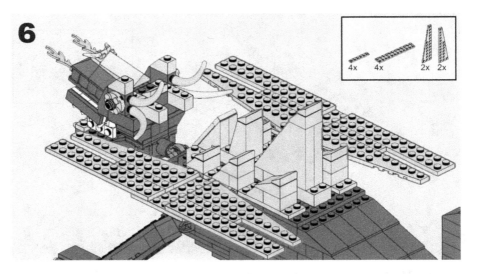

Figure 10-20. *Add on the wedge plate 12 × 3 and the 1 × 6 and 2 × 12 plates*

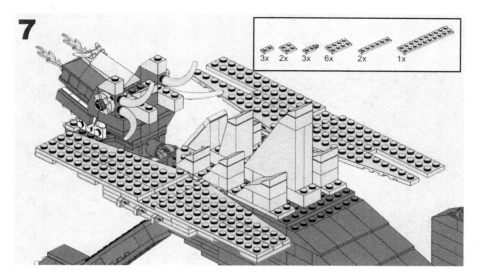

Figure 10-21. *Add on the plates and the 1 × 2 hinges*

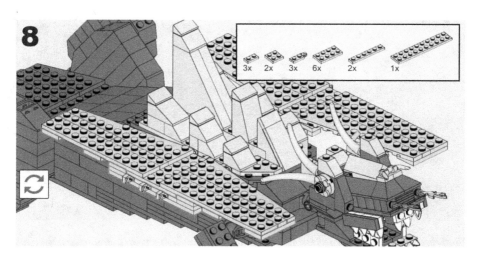

Figure 10-22. *Add on the plates and the 1 × 2 hinges*

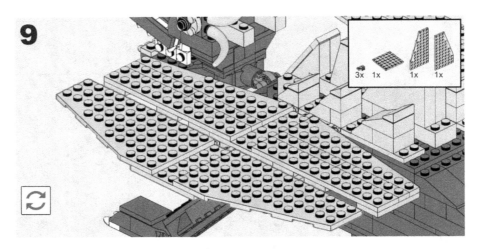

Figure 10-23. *Put on the 6 × 6 plates, the hinge plate 1 × 2, and the wedge plates 12 × 6 left and right*

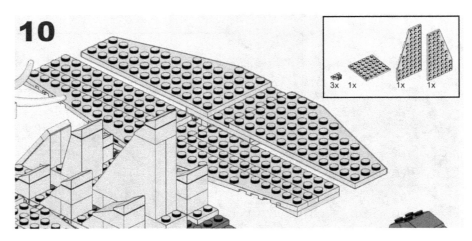

Figure 10-24. *Put on the 6 × 6 plates, the hinge plate 1 × 2, and the wedge plates 12 × 6 left and right*

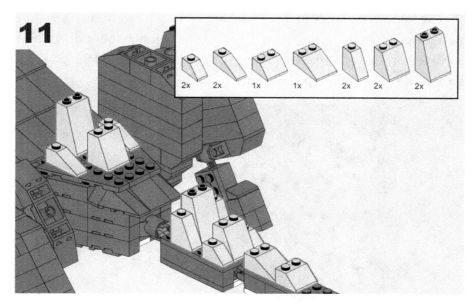

Figure 10-25. *Put on the slopes to help complete the back and tail of the dragon*

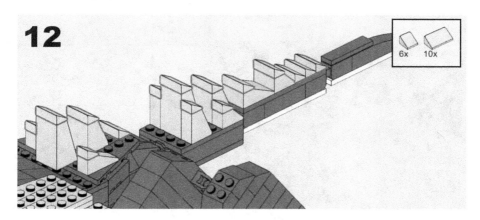

Figure 10-26. *Add on more slopes to complete the back and tail of the dragon*

The same rules apply to robots, as they can be posed in such a way that makes them dynamic and feel very lifelike, even though they are just parts put together. To do this, you are going to need to understand the power of diagonals, which I will explain later.

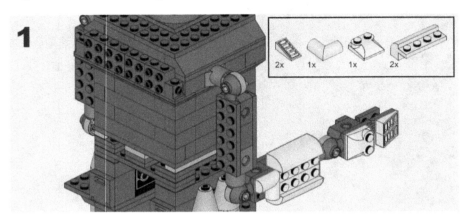

Figure 10-27. *Put on the slope 18 2 × 1 × 2/3 w/grille, the slope curved 2 × 2 × 2/3 (w/2 studs and curved sides), the slope curved 2 × 4 × 1 1/3, and the slope curved 2 × 2 × 2/3 double corner*

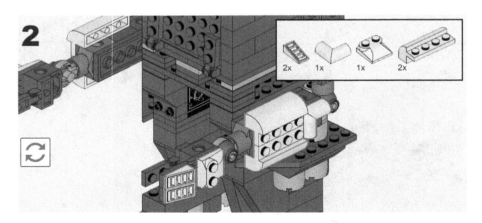

Figure 10-28. *Put on the slope 18 2 × 1 × 2/3 w/grille, the slope curved 2 × 2 × 2/3 (w/2 studs and curved sides), the slope curved 2 × 4 × 1 1/3, and the slope curved 2 × 2 × 2/3 double corner*

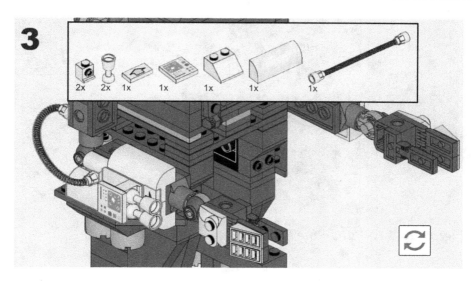

Figure 10-29. *Put on the brick modified 1 × 1 with headlight, the slope, the tiles, and the flexible hose*

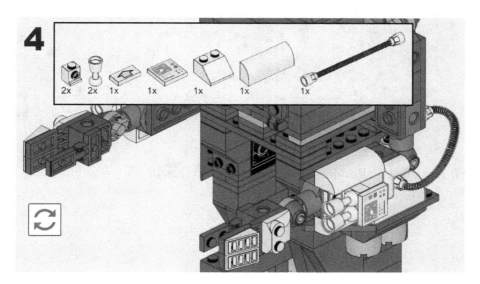

Figure 10-30. *Put on the brick modified 1 × 1 with headlight, the slope, the tiles, and the flexible hose*

321

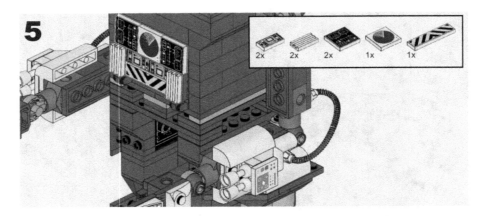

Figure 10-31. *Put on the tiles in front*

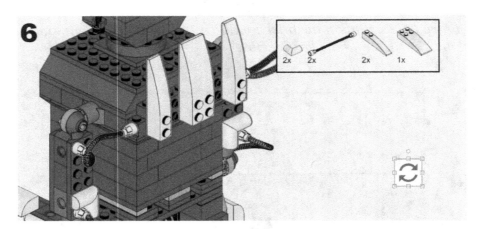

Figure 10-32. *Put on the curved slope 6 × 1 and 6 × 2 and the 2 × 2 × 2 × 3 double corner and then the hoses*

This is kind of a law of arts, and honestly, what I am attempting to do here is to create art. Things that are standing and vertical command attention, while things that are horizontal feel more passive. When things are on diagonals, it creates a sense of movement, like it comes alive.

I recommend a lot of tall things on a diorama, as well as things being as diagonal as possible without making them look ridiculous. It is the difference of seeing a photograph and seeing a video, and you want to create something that is essentially a world.

Okay, so now that I have created all this, I suppose I'm going to need to bring it all together in one place, so here it is, rendered in lovely Stud.io.

Figure 10-33. *All of the creations put in one place, with some duplication. It's not perfect, but it is by some stretch of the imagination*

Now, you might be looking at this and wondering: Why is there an airplane just sitting there? Why is the spaceship in the corner? Are the robot and dragon fighting?

Well, truth be told, I think I need to flush this story out. I'm guessing that if you have a massive LEGO project, such as a diorama of something that you like from some franchise, or maybe something that is altogether your own, you will be able to get some details right to make it come to life.

Tell you what. I will work on that, while you work on what you are working on.

Final Conclusion

I hope that this book has given you the motivation to start building LEGO worlds, and I highly recommend these different ways of creating.

1) Organize your pieces.

   If you are a huge LEGO fan, then you probably have scads of pieces that are left over from your childhood, and chances are, they might be in some box or storage tote of some kind. Once they all get collected there, they are usually sold off or just given away. This is an easy way to get more pieces for what you want to build.

   However, you are going to need to organize them, and I highly recommend some kind of sorting by their form or category, as illustrated in Chapter 1. How you want to do that is up to you, because personally, I like to have them in drawers, big and small, if this is possible.

   You'll find that organizing will give you a big picture of what pieces you do have so you can figure out the next logical step of what you can build. For what you can't build, this is where you can start ordering very specific pieces.

2) Plan it out as best you can.

Every building that you have ever been in has had blueprints, because when it comes to construction, there is very little room for spur-of-the-moment and improvisation. Nothing is more frustrating when building something in LEGO only to find that you just don't have enough pieces to complete what you need to create.

If you are going to do a very large project, I highly recommend getting a sheet of paper, or going to your paint program and really figuring out where to start from. From there, find a program like Stud.io to really start creating a model, or just get the pieces out and see if it will work. Unlike real construction work, LEGO allows for more improvisation, and it is sometimes the most unplanned things work the best.

3) Use building techniques that will keep your model together.

No matter what you build, you are going to need to have some kind of strong base, even if it is just a near-paper thin baseplate. Personally, I recommend that you create a very strong base that has plates on the bottom, bricks in the middle, and plates on top for maximum strength.

I also highly recommend a two-stud overlap when you need to make something stand strong. Any type of securing over that is also good for creating a construction so strong that it should hold.

4) With the minifigs as a standard, make a place where they could comfortably live.

If you are building anything where a minifig has to essentially live in, which includes a house, car, airplane, spaceship, and anything else, then that minifig has to be somewhat comfortable in that space. When it comes to a house, you are going to want to make rooms that are small enough to be contained, but at least wide enough so a LEGO minifig can stretch out its arms, even though most minifigs cannot stretch out their arms.

My point is not to create things like houses where there are no staircases joining the two floors. The way minifigs are constructed can often work against them, meaning they are harder to place in something that is confining, like a car and an airplane. Fortunately, there are ways around this, and the more you learn about this, the more you can make space efficiently work for you.

5) Building on a smaller scale is actually harder than the larger.

With LEGO, you are really creating a miniature world, but the scale can sometimes be a little off. Some of the smallest pieces in LEGO, such as a 1×1 plate, would actually be quite large (about the size of your hand or foot). With this in mind, you have to create things that will accommodate this scale, even though reality might not match it because life is full of small things.

Like working within the confines, LEGO offers some chance at building so something larger in scale can still come off as being lifelike in the world of LEGO minifigs. Take advantage of a lot of little pieces to create a lot of smaller scale projects.

6)   Even if you can't make a LEGO creation do what it needs to do, at least make it look like it could.

The best part about LEGO is how versatile the bricks can be. You can take a pile of bricks and compact them together and make a large rock, or you can spread out those bricks to be walls and make a house.

There is also another advantage as you can literally make a car and yet have no engine in it. Even the car that I created in this book has opening doors, but no way to make it go. Sometimes, it works better that way, and as a LEGO creator, you are going to have to decide what is important for your creation.

7)   Take legitimate shortcuts.

There is going to be times where you will want to create something with a lot of detail, and projects like that can be very time-consuming, especially when every brick needs to really add to the project. Then, there are times where you can just create something and copy it many times and produce the same effect.

Whatever you do, try and make something where legitimate shortcuts can be made and really go from there. I showed in Chapter 7 how easy it is to turn a frame of a Cessna into a helicopter, and there are times where you don't have to invent the wheel in your creation. My advice to this is: if you do copy or imitate, try and put your own spin on it, as LEGO is about continuous improvement.

8) Account for everything.

This is a difficult thing, because you have to really put your mind into that of a LEGO minifig. As I have said before, you want to insure that the LEGO minifig is comfortable, which is why I have instructions on how to make a LEGO toilet. You are going to have to figure out the needs of your LEGO minifig and build the model around that, to the point where it has access to the bathroom! Of course, there are limits to this, because you could build a LEGO grocery store, but as far as how it gets stocked, maybe it is time to stop the thinking and start creating.

9) Details matter, so take the time to get them right.

This entire chapter has been about creating details, and you probably have noticed how small things can make a big difference. If you put a lot of small things together, it can often change something ordinary into something extraordinary.

10)   Always be building and always be rebuilding.

There are times where you can be building, and it can get frustrating. I recommend taking breaks, short and long, and you can often come back rejuvenated and discover that what you were doing wasn't so bad after all.

There are times where you are building something and discover that you will have to rebuild it from the ground up. I highly recommend this, even though it is both time-consuming and possibly frustrating (especially if you have to do it again).

Anyway, that about concludes this book, and I am currently working on doing several videos based on what I discussed in this book. Keep your eyes peeled for that one, but for now, I'll use my signature signoff from my website and YouTube channel of TheGeekChurch.

This is Mark Rollins, and I am signing off.

Index

H, I, J

Helicopter
    Cessna, 228
    construction, 230–234
    LEGO Technic book, 228
    modified brick, 228
    pilots and passengers fit, 229
    reverse engineering, 228
    tail shuttle piece, 229
Hinges, 8, 53–55, 66, 254, 258
History of LEGO
    adventurers, 15
    basic sets, 9
    car models, 19
    creator, 4
    creator system, 18
    expert sets, 10
    Fabuland, 11
    girl-friendly models, 13
    Harry Potter, 17
    ice planet sets, 12
    island extreme sets, 17
    Knights Kingdom, 18
    knights system, 13
    LEGO family, 9
    licensed sets, 18
    light and sound, 12
    Maniac, 13, 14
    MINDSTORMS, 16
    minifig scale, 19
    MyBot system, 16
    new sets, 14, 15
    Ninjago, 18
    pirates collections, 12
    Prince of Persia sets, 18
    products, 18
    sets, 19, 59
    sets advances, 14
    space sets, 12
    space system, 10, 11
    Star Wars–related toys, 15
    The Lego Movie, 18
    town and knights sets, 16
    town sets, 9
    towns systems, 10, 13
    toys you grow up with, 11, 12
    wooden toys, 7
House, 109–159, 163, 182, 202, 240,
    258, 304–305, 326, 327

K

Kitchen counter
    construction, 168–171
Kitchen floor, 304

L

Landing gear, 240, 241, 243
Legitimate shortcuts, 327, 328
LEGO, 2
    Ad campaign, 12
    baseplates, 68, 69
    catalog, 5, 6, 8
    meaning, 5
    pieces, 59
    sets, 60

GPSR Compliance
The European Union's (EU) General Product Safety Regulation (GPSR) is a set
of rules that requires consumer products to be safe and our obligations to
ensure this.

If you have any concerns about our products, you can contact us on

ProductSafety@springernature.com

In case Publisher is established outside the EU, the EU authorized
representative is:

Springer Nature Customer Service Center GmbH
Europaplatz 3
69115 Heidelberg, Germany